Invitation to a Royal WEDDING

Invitation to a Royal WEDDING

EDWARD AND SOPHIE   JUNE 19, 1999

PETER DONNELLY

FOREWORD BY INGRID SEWARD

CLB

5157 Invitation to a Royal Wedding
Produced for Quadrillion Publishing by
Bookman Projects Ltd.,
Floor 22
Mirror Group
One Canada Square
London E14 5AP
England

This edition published in 1999 by CLB,
an imprint of Quadrillion Publishing Ltd

Distributed in the US by Quadrillion Publishing Inc.,
230 Fifth Avenue, NY, NY 10001

ISBN 1-84100-221-6

Printed and bound in Italy by G. Canale, Torino

Credits

For Bookman Projects Ltd:
Editor • Suzanne Evins
Consultant • Sean Smith
Design • Carl Panday
Picture Research • Christine Cornick
Colour Reproduction • John Symonds
Facilities • Ric Papineau
Publishing Director • Nick Kent

For Quadrillion Publishing Ltd:
Editorial Director • Will Steeds
Art Director • Phil Chidlow
Production Director • Graeme Procter
Additional design and editorial support: Bron Kowal, John O'Hara, Mary Ryan

CONTENTS

FOREWORD

Prince Edward and his bride Sophie Rhys-Jones are the epitome of a modern royal couple. They both have careers and work hard, yet have great respect for the institution of the monarchy and their homeland – Great Britain.

Prince Edward – Cambridge graduate, former Royal Marine, company director, television presenter and seventh in line to the throne – has the quiet confidence of one born to privilege. He is used to things being done his way, but the image the prince presents to the world bears very little reality to the real person. He is sensitive and intelligent, and less bound by tradition than any of his other siblings.

Calling himself Edward Windsor, he has chosen to break out of the royal mould set for him in early childhood and make his own way in life. But he is also aware of the responsibilities his royal position has thrust upon him and therefore his personal ambitions will always be tempered by loyalty to his family and his mother, the Queen.

The failure of the marriage of his sister Princess Anne and then in rapid succession those of his brothers Prince Andrew and Prince Charles, forced him to put caution before commitment when it came to finding a wife. He was raised to believe in family life – it is what the royal family stands for: a regal bulwark against the slippage of moral values and changing social mores.

By generations of tradition, royal marriages have been matters of dynastic or political expedience, dressed up as national celebrations. The last few decades, however, have seen them become public fairytales, which have then twisted into the stuff of nightmares.

Prince Edward has decided his marriage will not suffer this way. It took him five years to ask Sophie to be his bride and, having made the decision, he is determined it will work.

So is Sophie. She is ambitious and hard-working. She has to be. She does not have the financial backing or the aristocratic connections of Diana, Princess of Wales. Neither is she part of the jet-set, which played such an important part in Fergie's life. Aware the majority of people will never meet her and that their impressions will be formed by what they see on television and in magazines and newspapers, she has taken care not to be too flamboyant, and she has done it well.

She knows that what is acceptable for just about everyone else does not apply to royalty and she is aware of her responsibilities. It is a fraught and unparalleled situation that she, and almost anyone else who marries into the royal family, has to deal with. But deal with it she has.

Sophie is exactly the kind of woman Prince Edward wants to be with. He respects her and the feeling is mutual. She has had time to empathize with the family she has married into and understands the thousand years of history which is part of the monarchy, and is privileged to become a part of it.

Edward and Sophie are in love. They should be allowed the opportunity to be happy together. So let them step forward into the future with our blessing.

Ingrid Seward

Ingrid Seward
Editor-in-Chief, *Majesty* magazine

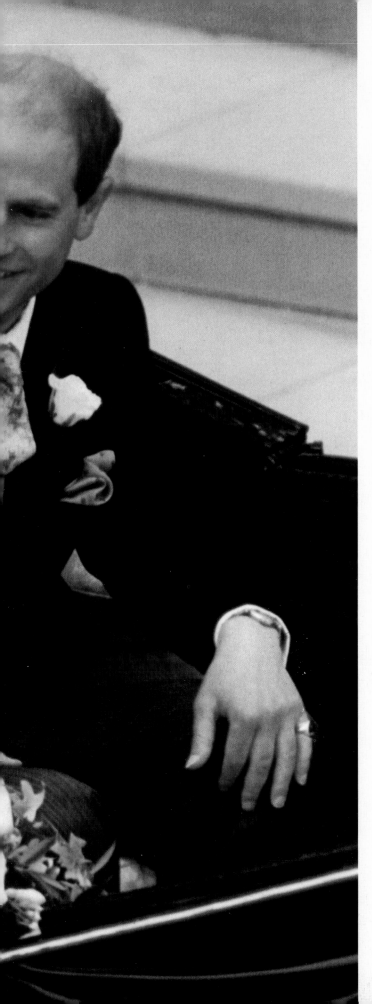

Chapter One

SO HAPPY TOGETHER

*Edward and Sophie
have their wish for
a country-style wedding*

———◆———

The marriage of Edward and Sophie was the last royal wedding of the 20th-century, and it was notable for its refreshingly modern style. It was an almost informal country-style wedding, with friends and family bussed in on mini-coaches to the chapel, and later they helped themselves at a relaxed buffet reception.

But Prince Edward and Sophie Rhys-Jones had to fight their corner to get the wedding they really wanted, and in the end came to a compromise with royal courtiers who insisted on at least a little ceremonial to keep up the image of the family Firm – to the delight of a worldwide television audience of some 200 million.

Tradition won again, when the bride and her groom emerged from St George's Chapel, Windsor, as the newly-created Earl and Countess of Wessex. But they made it plain in a television interview aired a few days before the wedding, that they still very much intended to go on as before, as Edward Windsor, TV producer, and Sophie Rhys-Jones, PR executive.

Sophie, though, was already adjusting to her new dual role, and in the hectic days before the wedding attended what was seen as her first royal duty – riding in a carriage with the Queen Mother at the Trooping the Colour ceremony in London and later appearing with Edward and members of his family on the balcony of Buckingham Palace.

Left: Smiling broadly, newlyweds Edward and Sophie – now the Earl and Countess of Wessex – leave for a short tour of Windsor in one of the Queen's horse-drawn landaus before joining their guests for the reception in St George's Hall.

"She admitted she was beginning to feel butterflies about the wedding"

The wedding, in the end, was the one they always wanted. Well almost. Prince Edward and Sophie Rhys-Jones had insisted from the start that they would love a quiet family wedding, in a place they both much admired and with just family and close friends there to wish them well. But that, they both knew even when they said it on their engagement day, would not be a popular move and seemed a highly unrealizable dream.

For with the marriage, the man who likes to be called Edward Windsor was taking public-relations executive Sophie Rhys-Jones into a world in which she would have to share the responsibilities of his other role, as a prince of the realm, to his mother the Queen, his country and the Commonwealth. And before long came steadily-increasing calls, not least from courtiers who look after the interests of the royal family – known as "The Firm" – for a wedding that the public could share.

After much discussion, during which the "tough cookie" businessman Edward argued his corner, and Sophie made it very clear what she would like, there was a canny compromise which produced, for the last royal wedding of the 20th century, one unlike any other ever seen in Britain, and it may well set the pattern for the future.

It *was* a family wedding in the English country-side, away from the pomp and pageantry of London's abbeys and cathedrals, with the smell of summer roses heavy in the air and the bridegroom and his brothers just strolling down to the chapel from their mother's home up the way. Friends came out to wave them off, relatives arrived by mini-bus – and didn't mind at all that there was just a buffet reception. "They achieved exactly what they wanted", British historian Robert Lacey beamed when it was all over. "It was just like a country wedding".

The fact that it was all watched by an estimated world-wide television audience of 200 million – and that the bride went in as Sophie Rhys-Jones and came out as the new Countess of Wessex – seemed almost incidental to the main purpose of the happy union of a modern, go-ahead couple with busy lives and demanding careers. And planning the wedding had been taking up a great deal of their valuable time since the engagement announcement in January. For Sophie, as for any bride, the days leading up to the wedding had become increasingly hectic.

Just eight days before the big occasion, she arrived with Edward at London's Guildhall for a charity dinner-dance in aid of the Duke of Edinburgh Award's International Association. Wearing a sequinned gown trimmed with green velvet, a shimmering green shawl, and diamond earrings and necklace (*and* that engagement ring) she had two dances with her husband-to-be – and laughed with him when a charity auctioneer invited bids for a holiday in New Zealand – "a smashing honeymoon location". She admitted to fellow

Above: Sophie poses with flowers outside her office after her last day at work.

Right: Only eight days to go, but Edward and Sophie are completely relaxed at the Guildhall dinner-dance.

guests that she was beginning to feel "butterflies in the stomach" about the wedding.

But there was no sign of nerves the next morning, when she arrived for her last day at work before the big occasion – and left in the evening carrying a bouquet of flowers presented to her by colleagues. At least the problem of flowers for the wedding had now been solved: Lavender Flowers of Windsor, who she had chosen to design the arrangements, said they had worked closely with Sophie and her dress designer to create an effect that would "mirror the stylish and romantic thoughts of the bride and groom".

That evening, Sophie watched on television as Prince Philip celebrated his 78th birthday by taking the salute on Horse Guards at a Beat Retreat performed by the Massed Bands of the Royal Marines. And on Saturday, just a week before the wedding, she was on show herself – making her first important appearance with the Royal Family at the Trooping the Colour ceremony.

This page: Sophie's first appearance on the balcony at Buckingham Palace (above), watching the Trooping the Colour. On the way to the ceremony (below), Sophie was honoured to be invited, with Edward, to ride in the Queen Mother's carriage.

Afterwards, she looked more relaxed as she appeared with members of the royal family on the famous balcony of Buckingham Palace – in marked contrast, observers said, to the 19-year-old Lady Diana Spencer, who seemed shy and nervous when she had made her debut appearance on the balcony in 1981.

An audience with the happy couple

Inevitably, the subject of Diana came up again the following day, when Edward and Sophie appeared in an exclusive TV interview with the BBC's Sue Barker – and they laughed when they talked about how she had been partly responsible for the couple first meeting.

Casually dressed and sitting in the grounds of their new home, Bagshot Park, Edward and Sophie talked of their lives, love and hopes for the future in an informal and often happy discussion – and said how delighted they were at the public response to the wedding.

"When we were asked what we were going to do", said the prince, " we said: 'Oh, just a nice quiet, family wedding if possible', thinking nobody's going to take any notice of this. But it's just got bigger and bigger. It's just brilliant!"

Even so, they still wanted to keep it as low-key as possible and to be seen as "an ordinary couple" with none of the media hysteria which surrounded Princess Diana.

Above: Edward chats to members of the Royal Scottish National Orchestra's String Quartet at Holyroodhouse, Edinburgh – his last pre-wedding public engagement.

Below: Preparing for the reception at St George's Hall.

Although the Queen Mother was said to have kept both former royal wives – the late Princess of Wales and the Duchess of York – at a distance, she went out of her way to invite Sophie to ride with her in her open carriage to the ceremony. Sitting opposite Edward for this first big public occasion, Sophie looked nervous but stylish in a shapely navy-blue Tomasz Starzewski suit and dramatic cream-and-navy hat.

> ## "They said how delighted they were at the public response to the wedding"

Edward was at his most passionate in the half-hour interview – which was sold around the world with profits going to the couple's favourite charities – when he talked about his own search for privacy. "The most precious thing anybody possesses is anonymity", he said. Of the accident which killed Princess Diana in Paris two years earlier, he commented: "It was only a matter of time before something really very nasty happened".

Sophie, when asked about being compared to Diana, said: "The comparison is something I have always had. I've often in the past done double takes when I've seen a picture of what I thought

AN ODE TO LOVE

The morning of the wedding saw the release of Andrew Motion's first offering as the new Poet Laureate and it was, he admitted, a baptism of fire.

Motion produced his "Epithalamium", a form of Ancient Greek poem or song to celebrate marriage, a little more than three weeks after his appointment, and confessed he wondered if he should produce one at all so soon. "I knew I would be damned if I did and damned if I didn't. So I thought here was a chance to say 'I accept the challenge and off we go'".

But he said he found the poem "very tough to write", the words hard to come, but in the end he finished it in a fortnight. His 12-line ode, subtitled "St George's Chapel, Windsor", hopefully reflected any young couple's feelings at the start of their life together – and included a plea to the Press not to intrude on the lives of the newlyweds.

Motion's worries about his new role are understandable. The title is bestowed by the monarch on a contemporary poet, whose traditional duties include writing odes on great national and royal occasions. But it is a hard act to follow: the first official Poet Laureate was John Dryden, who served between 1668 and 1688. Others have not been too keen to take the job.

William Wordsworth (who became an enthusiastic republican during a visit to revolutionary France in 1791–92) at first refused the post, because he did not feel like churning out "instant" poems for royal occasions. He accepted in 1843, only after being promised he did not have to write a word if he did not want to – a condition which still applies!

Wordsworth was succeeded in 1850 by Alfred, Lord Tennyson, mainly because Queen Victoria and Prince Albert admired his "In Memoriam". He was the most successful Poet Laureate – although neither of his best-known laureate poems, "The Charge of the Light Brigade" and "Ode on the Death of the Duke of Wellington" are on royal subjects.

After the best came arguably the worst: Victoria appointed Alfred Austin in 1896, four years after Tennyson's demise, and he held the title until his death in 1913. He is remembered for the hysterical – rather than historical – lines he penned when bulletins reporting the illness of the Prince of Wales, later Edward VII, were issued via the newfangled telegraph system:

Across the wires the electric
message came;
He is no better, he is much
the same.

More recent laureates have included John Masefield (1930–68), Cecil Day-Lewis (1968–72), John Betjeman (1972–84) and Ted Hughes (1984-1998), who was followed in May 1999 by Andrew Motion.

The choice of Motion, Professor of Creative Writing at the University of East Anglia, Norwich, was widely regarded as a victory for tradition over the champions of a "poet of the people". But in a break with tradition, he was appointed for a fixed term of ten years, rather than being given the job for life. He said: "I want to write more than has been the pattern in the past. A laureate's work should always be something special, and the ten years will stop me over-staying my welcome".

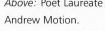

Above: Poet Laureate Andrew Motion.

Epithalamium
St George's Chapel, Windsor

One day, the tissue-light through stained glass falls
on vacant stone, on gaping pews, on air
made up of nothing more than atom storms
which whiten slowly, then disappear.

The next, all this is charged with brimming life.
A people-river floods those empty pews,
and music-torrents break – but then stop dead
to let two human voices make their vows:

to work – so what is true today remains the truth;
to hope – for privacy and what its secrets show;
to trust – that all the world can offer it will give;
to love – and what it has to understand to grow.

was either me or the Princess of Wales, and actually from a distance not knowing who it was until coming up close.

"On an aesthetic basis, I don't think anybody can be unhappy at being compared to somebody such as her. She was incredibly beautiful, but it's two very different people. She had her personality and I have mine".

Edward, referring to remarks that Sophie could not fill the gap left by Diana, insisted: "It's not helpful, it's not accurate. The princess was a completely unique person and what she did was tremendous. But the emotions she set in motion couldn't be controlled in any way".

The future Countess of Wessex

So what will Sophie's role be now? "I certainly see it more in a supporting role to Edward rather than rushing off and forging my own path and taking on the mantle of various different charities", she said. They were both busy with their careers, which they certainly mean to continue, and: "There is the Queen and the rest of the royal family doing an exceptionally wonderful job in a public role anyway and I don't see a massive need for me to go out there and do the same thing".

This page: Happy crowds lining Castle Hill (above) and Windsor High Street lend the "family occasion" an informal, carnival atmosphere – just as Edward and Sophie had wanted. Before the service (below),

there was a special treat for the spectators: seeing the bridegroom walk down Castle Hill from Windsor Castle to St George's Chapel with his two best men, brothers Prince Charles and Prince Andrew.

The challenges facing her? "Making our marriage work", said Sophie, although children were not in their immediate thoughts at the moment. "Contrary to public opinion", she added, repeating a phrase she used on her engagement day, "we actually haven't ever lived with each other before. So, you know, we want to get used to living with each other. There still will be an awful lot of things to do in the house and the garden and obviously with our respective businesses". Those who thought they should go straight into extending the family would just have to "wait patiently".

"A couple determined to establish a life distinct from the traditional royal model"

The interview was well-received, in Britain and abroad. "Here were two people embarking on the rest of their lives with few illusions", royal commentator Robert Hardman wrote in *The Daily Telegraph*. "There was none of the shy naïvety which accompanied the engagement of the Prince and Princess of Wales, nor the cosy tactility displayed by the Duke and Duchess of York. Instead, we saw a couple in their mid-30s, determined to establish a family life distinct from the traditional royal model while respecting royal duty. It was a polished performance, as one would expect from two people who work in the media".

After the interview, Edward headed off to royal engagements in Scotland, and Sophie disappeared to get on with the final preparations – although one report said she'd quietly flown to Italy with a friend to get a suntan for her big day. But she was back the day before the wedding, walking hand-in-hand with Edward from St George's Chapel, Windsor, in a dress rehearsal, wearing black jeans and a length of cream material knotted loosely round her waist to imitate her bridal train.

Next day it would be the real thing, with everything just as Edward and Sophie had planned from the start. And the world would see a royal wedding unlike any that had gone before …

Right: The bride's simple but stunning dress – decorated with no less than 325,000 cut-glass and pearl beads – drew gasps of admiration from guests when she entered the chapel.

Chapter Two

FOLLOW THAT DREAM

Sophie and Edward's wedding could set the style for future royal marriages

———❖———

E dward and Sophie wanted their wedding to be a family occasion – and many were sure it could at last bring a royal marriage that would not end in grim disappointment and public disenchantment.

Edward, in particular, was well aware of the importance of setting the right tone for the wedding of the year. He watched with the rest of the world while his sister and two brothers exchanged wedding vows with their chosen partners amid scenes of great pomp, tradition and joy, only to witness the horror of discord and separation as each marriage ended in divorce.

He has been acutely sensitive to the Queen's own sadness, as a devoted mother looking on helplessly while the marriages of Anne, Andrew and Charles all crumbled. She was brought up in a plainly devoted family and her own marriage has happily spanned six decades.

Realizing the serious damage three broken marriages have inflicted on the image of the royal family, the Queen has allowed her youngest son all the time he needs to be sure he has made the right choice – and is delighted that Sophie Rhys-Jones is the woman with whom he wants to spend the rest of his life.

With a wedding to herald the new millennium, they could well set the example for royal marriages in the years to come.

Left: At last they can share their "open secret" – and the joy is clear on the faces of Prince Edward and Sophie Rhys-Jones as they pose for the cameras in the garden of St James's Palace following the announcement of their engagement.

"Edward was convinced he had made the right choice"

Royal weddings throughout history have provided days of pomp and pageantry, colour and countrywide celebration and, when regal unions cemented alliances between nations and states, jubilation and diplomatic joy across borders and continents. And if royal marriages, as Queen Victoria famously declared, are a lottery, Prince Edward and Sophie Rhys-Jones were not only fabulously fortunate in finding each other, but also far-sighted and wise.

By taking his time on the question of marriage – far too long for some members of the Press and public – Edward was convinced he had made the right choice of partner to share his life in the full

Right: As their own "big day" rapidly approaches, Edward and Sophie step out together to attend the wedding of television presenter Catrina Skepper and Alessandro Guerrini Maraldi, in April 1999.

glare of the royal limelight. Sophie was equally convinced. Quashing suggestions that she had sometimes despaired of Edward ever popping the question during their five-year courtship, she declared: "I've never issued ultimatums", and as for joining the royal family: "It is slightly nerve wracking. But I'm ready for it now and I'm fully aware of the responsibilities and commitments".

A royal lottery

Others, less level-headed, have lived to regret entering the royal marriage lottery in which the prize is sometimes not worth the wager. The wayward future King George IV, persuaded into a match with Caroline of Brunswick on the strength of her portrait, all but fainted at first sight and smell of his bride-to-be, a slovenly, highly excitable and compulsive chatterbox with little interest in bathing or changing her underclothes. "I am not well", George moaned after very swiftly embracing her at their first meeting. "Pray get me a glass of brandy". Nor was Caroline impressed with the antics of the massively overweight Prince of Wales. "My God! Does the Prince always behave like that?", she asked. "I think he's very fat – and nothing like as handsome as his portrait!"

Their marriage, one of the most ill-fated in the history of the British monarchy, began with a shambolic wedding in the Chapel Royal at St James's Palace on April 8, 1795 – Caroline chattered incessantly to anyone who would listen and George seemed in a stupor after a night's heavy drinking – and was all but over when he continued to drown his sorrows in drink and threw up in a fireplace, where he soundly slept away his honeymoon night.

Queen Victoria's own marriage to her Saxe Coburg cousin Albert was, as she made the world aware, blissfully happy. "Oh", she wrote, after he accepted *her* proposal, "to feel I was, and am, loved by such an angel as Albert was too great a delight to describe. Oh! How I adore and love him I cannot say". Albert responded by declaring himself "in body, in soul, ever your slave" and proved a devoted husband and father who helped raise the image of the monarchy (and, incidentally, left the enduring legacy of the Christmas tree, introduced from his native Germany).

Of Victoria and Albert's nine children, according to Elizabeth (the Countess of) Longford, author of the biography *Victoria RI*, at least five had happy marriages, and "one clear proposition seems to emerge from these Victorian statistics: marriages arranged by and for those who know the rules, and contracted by those who keep them, are likely to succeed".

For proof, look only to the marriage of Prince Edward's own grandparents, King George VI and Lady Elizabeth Bowes-Lyon, the current Queen Mother. Their union and exemplary conduct helped limit the potentially destructive effects of the 1936 abdication crisis, when George's brother, Edward VIII, quit his throne for the love of American divorcee Wallis Simpson. The new king and queen gave the monarchy enhanced respect and, with daughters Elizabeth and Margaret, strongly emphasized the image of the royal family as close, loving and happy.

Similarly, the marriage of Edward's parents, which has spanned six decades, is as "rock solid" now, say friends, as it was when the young Princess Elizabeth married her third cousin Lieutenant Philip Mountbatten in November 1947. Elizabeth was just 13 years old when she was captivated by the handsome, blond 18-year-old naval cadet, who was charged with looking after the princess during a tour of Dartmouth Naval College in 1939.

Theirs may not have been an arranged marriage, but Philip has said: "If you spend ten minutes thinking about it – and a lot of people spent a great deal more time thinking about it – how many obviously eligible young men were available?" Their wedding, at Westminster Abbey, provided a joyous and glittering royal occasion to relieve grim post-war austerity in Britain. Despite strict rationing, the bride was given an extra 100 clothing coupons for her silk dress, although, in keeping with those still-tough times, the couple opted for a stay-at-home honeymoon at Broadlands, the Hampshire home of the family's beloved "Uncle Dickie" Mountbatten, and on the royal Balmoral estate in the tranquil Highlands of Scotland.

Above right: King George VI and his family pictured at home in Buckingham Palace in 1946. The supportive and devoted husband and wife were a source of inspiration for the British nation during World War II.

Below right: The union of Princess Elizabeth and Philip Mountbatten in 1947 has been another successful alliance, at a time when the choice of partners fit for a future queen was considered limited.

Above: Despite their many tribulations, the royal family remain close and devoted at heart. To mark the Queen Mother's 98th birthday, they pose for photographs outside Clarence House. Edward chats happily to his niece Zara Phillips.

Below: At the time of her marriage to Prince Andrew in 1986, Sarah Ferguson seemed like a breath of fresh air. But it wasn't long before the Palace had misgivings about her suitability as a duchess.

Thrust all too soon on to the Throne on the death of her father in 1952, the 25-year-old Queen Elizabeth II ushered in a "new Elizabethan age" which saw the abolition of what are today regarded as absurd anachronisms of royal life. These included the presentation of debutantes at Court and royalty's head-in-the-sand refusal to acknowledge divorced people, even denying innocent parties of divorce access to the Royal Enclosure at Ascot race meetings.

Monarchy and modern marriage

So when the marriages of three of her four children ended in divorce, the Queen reacted like any other concerned parent – with great sadness and self-searching doubts – but also with the added pain of knowing the image of the royal family had been severely dented. Like her husband, she remains strongly traditionalist, insisting that what was good enough for her generation should be good enough for the young. Her whole life has been dedicated to the ideal of duty and sacrifice before self, and even as divorce rates soar, the Queen finds it difficult to accept that the notion of a lifelong commitment to mother should be considered by some to be almost comically old-fashioned.

As a young princess, in 1949, she warned: "We live in an age of growing self-indulgence, of hardening materialism, and of falling moral standards. Some of the very principles on which the family is founded are in danger".

"Where", the Queen asked a friend, echoing the pain of many parents, "did we go wrong?"

She frequently stressed in her Christmas broadcasts the value of family life and, celebrating 25 years on the throne during her Silver Jubilee in 1977, declared that marriage "must be held firm in the web of family relationships – between parents and children, grandparents and grandchildren, cousins, aunts and uncles".

In recent times, as she has seen the marriages of three of her own children swept, one by one, on to the rocks, she realized that her own parents' idea of "The Firm" – as the royal family became known – as a model family setting an example to others, had been shipwrecked, too. "Where", the Queen asked a friend, echoing the puzzled pain of many parents throughout her realm, "did we go wrong?"

Even by current sombre statistics it was, for just one family, a sad and sorry catalogue of marital disharmony and divorce. There was Anne, the Princess Royal, widely considered the most down-to-earth and hard-working of the royals and the first of the Queen's children to marry. That marriage, to Captain Mark Phillips at Westminster Abbey in November 1973, produced children Peter and Zara, but finally ended after 15 years in September 1989.

Andrew, Duke of York, also married at the Abbey, in 1986. But his marriage to Sarah Ferguson was marred by a succession of scandals involving the flamboyant flame-haired "Fergie". There were sensational stories of her romances, financial affairs, book deals and other money-making enterprises, which embarrassed the royal family. The couple separated in March 1992 and were formally divorced in 1996, although they continued to share a home and holidays with their children, the princesses Beatrice and Eugenie.

The fairytale princess

Most significantly, there was Prince Charles, whose marriage to the young Lady Diana Spencer produced a showcase wedding of an Heir to the Throne, brilliantly stage-managed with that special style at which the British excel. Even the sun made a brief guest appearance during a dismal British summer as the couple were united on July 29, 1981, in what has been called the most public wedding in history. The archetypal "blushing bride" was a shy 19-year-old, who the world fell in love with on that magical day. Even the man who married them, the Archbishop of Canterbury, described the event as "the stuff of fairytales".

Above: Princess Anne ushered in a new generation of royal weddings when she married Capt. Mark Phillips. Fifteen years later she ushered in the first modern royal divorce.

Below: The most famous royal mismatch of them all. The nation had so many hopes for their Prince Charming and his bride when they married in 1981.

Above: The Prince and Princess of Wales were a divided couple, but they were still united in their love for their two sons William and Harry.

Right: The Queen's sombre dress reflected her mood during the *annus horribilis* of 1992, as Charles and Diana announced their separation.

Below: The fire at Windsor Castle was the ultimate blow for the beleaguered royal family, but somehow their public esteem has risen again from the ashes.

Looking back on that day, Diana recalled: "I thought I was the luckiest girl in the world when I looked at Charles through my veil. I had tremendous hope in my heart. At the age of 19 you always think you're prepared for anything, and you think you know what's coming".

The guest list was a mightily impressive roll call of aristocracy and politicians: every member of the British royal family; Princess Grace of Monaco; the Prince and Princess of Liechtenstein; the Grand Duke and Duchess of Luxembourg; the Queen and Prince Claus of the Netherlands; the King and Queen of Sweden; the Queen and Prince of Denmark; the King, Crown Prince and Princess of Norway; the King and Queen of the Belgians; the King of Tonga; French President François Mitterand; America's First Lady Nancy Reagan; and last, but certainly not least, British Prime Minister Margaret Thatcher.

Every last detail was noted when the bride, stunning in a sensational gown with a 25-foot (7.62-metre) train, walked down a red carpet stretching 652 feet (198 metres) to the High Altar in front of 3,500 guests and a phalanx of 22 television cameras covering the occasion for a massive audience (some 1,000 million in more than fifty countries). Ironically, the grand ceremony took place at St Paul's Cathedral, Christopher Wren's architectural masterpiece which looms over Fleet Street, historic home of the newspapers which would play a major role in publicizing the marital battles lying so close ahead. Those newspapers recorded Charles and Diana's every indiscretion and personal revelation. Despite the joy brought by the birth of their sons William and Harry, cracks appeared in the marriage, they separated and ultimately divorced.

Black November

The announcement of their separation came at the end of a bleak year for the monarchy. On November 20, 1992, the Queen watched, "devastated", according to Prince Andrew, as fire swept through treasured sections of Windsor Castle, where she and sister Margaret had shared so many idyllic

hildhood days – St George's Hall, the Queen's rivate chapel, the Brunswick Tower. It was followed y an unseemly public row over who would pay the stimated £60 million repair bill.

On November 23, at a London Guildhall lunch o mark her 40th year on the Throne, the Queen ave what Elizabeth Longford called "the most ompletely unforgettable speech of her reign". In a oice hoarse from a severe cold, which emphasized er anguish, she told of her *annus horribilis* and, vhile accepting that all institutions, including the nonarchy, must expect criticism, appealed for it to e tempered with "a touch of gentleness, good umour and understanding".

Two days later Prime Minister John Major told he House of Commons that, at the Queen's wish, he and Prince Charles were to start paying income ax like any other British citizen. Only three nembers of The Firm – the Queen, Prince Philip nd the Queen Mother – would "claim expenses" rom the state on the Civil List. The Queen would tow pay, from her own private income, those of Anne, Andrew, Edward and Princess Alice, Duchess f Gloucester.

> ## "I thought I was the luckiest girl in the world when I looked at Charles. I had tremendous hope in my heart"

Soon afterwards, on December 9, John Major vas on his feet again in parliament to announce, fter months of speculation, the separation of Charles and Diana. "The Queen and the Duke of Edinburgh, though saddened", he read, "understand and sympathize with the difficulties hat have led to the decision", and they hoped that ntrusions into the couple's privacy would now stop, so they could give their children a happy and secure upbringing.

There was, though, a happy end to the Queen's *annus horrilibis* – with a royal wedding. On December 12, just three days after the world had been told of Prince Charles' separation, Anne, the Princess Royal, married her second husband, Royal Navy Commander Timothy Laurence, in a very modest ceremony in Craithie Church at Balmoral.

Princess Anne remarries

It was, said observers, a shrewd move. The Queen's daughter had not remarried in an English church, but quietly in Scotland – a country for which Anne has a deep affection. She sent her children to Gordonstoun, the Morayshire public school attended by her father and brothers, and is a patron of the Scottish Rugby Union – son Peter represented Scotland in international schools rugby – and often turns up to cheer on the Scots in their

Below: A wistful Diana, Princess of Wales, faces the world on the day of her divorce in August 1996. Edward and Sophie would have to wait before the public would be ready for another royal marriage.

SAILING INTO THE SUNSET

The royal honeymoon yacht
Britannia *weighs her final anchor*

It seems the dream honeymoon of every bride – being whisked away on a private yacht and into a happy ever after. But the marriages of four of the Queen's family ended in divorce after they honeymooned on the royal yacht *Britannia*. First sister Margaret with Lord Snowdon, then Princess Anne with Captain Mark Phillips, Charles with Lady Diana Spencer, and Andrew with Sarah Ferguson.

So it was with mixed emotions that Edward and Sophie joined his family at Portsmouth naval docks in December 1997, to bid farewell to *Britannia*. The grand old yacht was due to sail gracefully into retirement in Scottish waters, after almost 44 years' service as the Queen's floating home-away-from-home and the world's most luxurious royals-only honeymoon hotel.

Above: The proud bows of the *Britannia* rest at anchor. Her days escorting newlyweds as a royal "love boat" are now over.

Opposite, bottom right: The Queen, flanked by Prince Philip and Prince Charles, wipes away an emotional tear during *Britannia*'s wintry decommissioning ceremony.

Opposite, top right: After sharing many holidays on the yacht, Edward and Sophie join the sad farewell.

It was in 1953, her Coronation year, that the Queen smashed a bottle of champagne over the Clyde-built vessel and gave her the name she and Prince Philip had chosen together. For the couple, *Britannia* was always special, because all their other homes – Buckingham Palace, Windsor, Balmoral, Sandringham – had been built and occupied by others. "But", Philip has recalled, "we were involved with *Britannia* from the very beginning". Even, it has been said, from his objecting to the initial design of the state rooms and being overruled by the Admiralty. ("He can change the colour of the lampshades", was their reported response.)

Britannia *rules the waves*

The 413-foot (126-metre) yacht, crewed by 19 officers and 217 men and based on the design of a cross-Channel steamer, had proudly flown the flag for Britain throughout the world. She had played host to politicians and celebrities on many glittering occasions during the Queen's state visits abroad. Now, however, the ship was becoming increasingly costly to maintain and had almost reached the end of her useful life. Even so, Edward argued vociferously that she should keep her status as royal yacht, because she helped bring in business: "No other country in the world has anything to match *Britannia*", he said. "She is a symbol of Britain".

His sister Anne, on the other hand, agreed with many navy officials who wanted to see *Britannia* scuttled. But in the end, the ship's final fate rested with the British government, who decided she should be saved: "*Britannia* has a special place in the people's affections", said Defence Secretary George Robertson. "This was con-

firmed by the many thousands who turned out to see her around the country on her final tour".

Interested parties were invited to submit proposals for *Britannia's* future, and of the nine tenders the prize went to the Forth Ports Authority in Scotland, with plans to make the yacht an exhibition and conference centre, the "jewel in the crown" of Edinburgh's £50 million waterside development at Leith.

At *Britannia's* farewell, Prince Philip swallowed hard and the Queen blinked away tears as the Royal Marine band played "Sunset" and the royal standard and white ensign were slowly lowered. An era came to a close with the sounds of "Rule Britannia" as the Queen, head of a once-great naval power, became its first monarch in 330 years without the use of a personal sea-faring vessel.

For her family, too, it was an emotional time. Not least for Prince

Charles, with memories of his honeymoon with Diana, during which she is said to have been upset at having to share meals with naval officers *and* that Royal Marine band. For Edward, grim-faced as he and Sophie watched the sad farewell, there would be no such start. But as they embarked on their own life together, they knew they had taken their time and set fair for calmer waters.

Above: Princess Anne had learnt a hard lesson by the time of her second marriage to Commander Tim Laurence. With not a gilded carriage in sight, she chose a private wedding in Craithie Church at Balmoral.

Right: The marriage of Princess Anne and Tim Laurence has flourished away from the public gaze, where they prefer to exist without the more glamorous trappings afforded to royalty.

big matches. There were even suggestions that she may be made a "princess regent" in Scotland, to help maintain the unity of her mother's realm in a devolved Britain.

Her "quiet" wedding, the first recent royal ceremony to depart from pomp and pageantry, still created massive media interest, with a Press pack of more than 200 descending on the Queen's "quiet country retreat". Among them was Tom Rhodes, then a reporter for *The Times*, who recalls: "It was quite farcical in a way, because they were determined to keep it all as private as possible.

"Police and royal estate staff stopped cameramen and reporters getting anywhere near, and the workers were so incredibly loyal to the royal family that they would not tell you even the tiniest thing. It was like a sort of Scottish *omertà*, the Sicilian rule of silence". Approaching one worker at the gates of Balmoral, Rhodes was told: "We never talk about Her Majesty – and I hope we never will", and he duly reported that "a silence to rival that of the Mafia in the face of a media invasion" had descended on the royal estate.

"But of course Anne's wedding still received worldwide media coverage", adds Rhodes, who now works for *The Sunday Times* in New York, "and there is huge interest in America in the royal family. Edward's TV programmes are shown here, and when his engagement was announced it got blanket coverage throughout the US".

Changing styles

With such intense interest at home and abroad, there seemed little chance that Edward and Sophie's hopes for a relatively quiet wedding would be realized. She said: "I think getting married is a very personal thing" and the prince, asked what sort of wedding he would like, replied: "A family one, hopefully. I think there is no such thing as a private wedding, but I hope that it will be predominantly a family wedding". A modest affair? "Yes, I think so", he said, before smiling: "I expect I'm going to be deeply unpopular".

"*I hope that it will be predominantly a family wedding*"

Surprising as it may seem today, at one time all royal weddings were held away from the public gaze – in the private chapels of castles and palaces and with only close family and friends plus officials of state allowed to watch the proceedings, which were often brief and businesslike. The first public royal wedding was in 1501, when Arthur, Prince of Wales, married Catherine of Aragon.

Massive crowds (more than 100,000, according to royal census-takers) cheered the bride as her procession of carriages trotted from Westminster Palace through the streets of London to St Paul's Cathedral, where a raised wooden platform outside the main entrance was covered with a white carpet to protect Catherine's white and cloth-of-silver gown from the mud. Afterwards there was a huge banquet of extravagant dishes served on gold plate, followed by a public bedding for the couple and dancing for their guests.

When Arthur died soon afterwards and his brother, Henry VIII, married his widow, it was a strictly private affair at Greenwich – and although every British schoolchild knows that he married six times ("two divorced, two beheaded, one died, one survived") and Henry revelled in public displays, all the ceremonies were similarly quiet occasions and royal weddings once again became private concerns.

In more recent times, the wedding of another Prince of Wales, the future King Edward VII, to Princess Alexandra of Denmark, was meant to be a comparatively quiet occasion in St George's Chapel, Windsor, on March 10, 1863. His mother Queen Victoria, still grieving for her late husband Albert, stayed above it all and ordered daughter Vicky to keep the celebrations restrained.

The public, though, were out for fun, and when the couple's carriage drove through Windsor on the first stage of their honeymoon journey to the Isle of Wight, crowds broke through police cordons to wish them good luck. Eton schoolboys – including Winston Churchill's father Randolph – were given the day off lessons to celebrate, and joined the mobs causing pandemonium on the Queen's highways. More chaos ensued as a train laid on to take VIP guests back into London was over-run by crowds, and dukes and duchesses, lords and ladies, found themselves sharing carriages with "common" people.

George V, Prince Edward's great-grandfather, was married privately in the Chapel Royal at St James's Palace in 1893, but three of his six children had very public weddings at Westminster Abbey. Not least of these was the Duke of York, whose wedding in April 1923 introduced his beautiful bride ("a vision of loveliness" in her medieval-style gown of satin and lace) to the nation she continues to captivate as the Queen Mother.

Above: Queen Victoria, flanked by the Prince of Wales and Princess Alexandra. Despite her reputation for a stiff upper lip, she enjoyed a blissful marriage and headed a happy family.

Opposite: When the Duke of York married Lady Elizabeth Bowes-Lyon in Westminster Abbey in 1923, they never dreamed they would one day be king and queen. The bride laid her wedding bouquet on the tomb of the unknown soldier before walking down the aisle.

With the birth of television, vast new audiences were allowed to share the spectacle of a royal wedding, and Princess Margaret's 1960 marriage to Lord Snowdon was the first seen by millions. But by then her sister had already learned the power of the new medium. It was Queen Elizabeth II, against the advice of Prime Minister Winston Churchill, his cabinet and the Archbishop of Canterbury, who had insisted that her Coronation on June 2, 1953, should be televised – a hugely popular move which even in those early days of television drew an audience of some 20 million.

Happily ever after …

Compared to that, even a royal wedding was a far less important affair, and there was some feeling that Edward and Sophie's desire to keep their wedding quiet – or as quiet as possible – was a sensible one and that perhaps the time for a change had come. "Wisely, the engaged couple opted for a more muted ceremony", wrote royal author Alison Weir in *The Independent* newspaper. "They have returned to the tradition established by their forebears in an age when marriage was taken more seriously. It is encouraging that, in an era obsessed with the superficial, Edward and Sophie have indicated their wish to accord substance precedence over style, and are perhaps setting a new trend for royal weddings".

Edward's hopes of keeping his marriage low-key seemed to be reflected in the restrained media interest in the couple and the "big event" in the run-up to the wedding. This followed a general feeling within the nation that it was time a member of the royal family had a romance which could end with a "happily ever after", and a marriage which could stand the test of time.

The omens, many pointed out, were good: both bride and groom were of an age to know their own minds – Edward at 35 the Queen's youngest son but the oldest to marry, and Sophie just 10 months younger. Both had been out and about in the world

Below: Princess Margaret's beautiful Norman Hartnell wedding dress was the centrepiece of the first royal wedding of the television age. Closed-circuit TV in Westminster Abbey reached an estimated world-wide audience of 320 million.

enjoyed absorbing careers and had taken the time to get to know each other well – although Sophie made a point of saying that, despite popular perception, she and Edward did not live together, and never had.

"It is encouraging they wish to accord substance and precedence over style"

Most importantly, though, she has a happy family background. Unlike Lady Diana Spencer and Sarah Ferguson, who both came from uppercrust but broken homes, Sophie's family is solid, stable, ordinary English middle-class – so ordinary that her father, Christopher, shared the common concerns of many another father-of-the-bride. Who was going to pay for even a "private" royal wedding was his chief worry when he lunched with leading British journalist Nigel Dempster, not long before the engagement was publicly announced.

Nor was Mr Rhys-Jones the only one to worry about the approaching nuptials. A leading article in *The Guardian* whinged: "The spirit should soar in joyful anticipation of it all. Why is it, then, that dread clutches at the heart?" Edward, the newspaper argued, has no significant constitutional role: "There is no magic. So spare us the sentimentality this time round".

Happily, not many cast such funereal gloom over what should be the most joyful day of any young couple, and the *Daily Telegraph* rejoiced: "There have been clouds over the realm of royal marriages long enough for this glint of sunshine to be gladly received". But, recalling a remark of the 16th-century French statesman the Duc de Sully that "the English take their pleasures sadly, after the fashion of their country", the newspaper warned that there would be lists of questions about the marriage: "Why did he take so long to propose? How will they live with the strain of previous failed royal marriages? Can a princess also remain a businesswoman?"

All those questions, it concluded, would be soberly posed in the days ahead. "How much nicer it would be for them, and for us, if we could bring ourselves to set all the solemn questions to one side and sincerely wish them a happy married life".

And so said many millions more.

This page: Prince Edward has always envied the way his cousins Lady Sarah Armstrong-Jones and Viscount Linley have managed to find happiness and privacy in equal measures. As a guest at both Sarah's wedding to Daniel Chatto (right) and David Linley's wedding to Serena Stanhope (below), Edward was able to formulate plans for his own wedding to Sophie.

Chapter Three

JUST CALL ME EDWARD WINDSOR

A young man who is quiet and reserved by nature, but is determined to do his own thing

A s the Queen's youngest son and a member of the most photographed family in the world, Prince Edward has had to learn many of life's lessons in the unrelenting glare of public scrutiny.

From an early age, he has tried to achieve the nearly impossible for someone in his supremely privileged position – to mingle with the crowd. It is a tribute to his strength of character and dedication that he has, on the whole, been able to set his own agenda in life.

He survived the austere regime of Gordonstoun, where elder brother Charles had such a difficult time, and won a place at Cambridge, despite only average academic grades. After university, a traditional royal career in the armed forces beckoned. But Edward bravely turned his back on the Royal Marines, facing a host of public and Press sneering, before ultimately winning respect by being successful in his chosen career in theatre and television, a world he knew and loved.

He has followed a similar, determined course in his private life, becoming fiercely protective of his girlfriends. His refusal to be rushed into marriage is just one example of his robust attitude. He has always been his own man, a quality Sophie much admires.

Left: Prince Edward has always been relaxed in front of the camera, a quality that has served him well in his recent television career. His love of theatre and acting has helped him overcome a natural shyness.

"He is the first to break away from royal routine and ritual"

Top right: From a young age Edward showed a natural aptitude for riding, a sport he now enjoys with Sophie.

Below: Edward (right) helps brother Andrew maintain the Palace grounds. The two boys formed the Queen's "second family".

His Royal Highness Prince Edward Antony Richard Louis sometimes says: "Just call me Edward … Edward Windsor", and although he also uses the name in business correspondence and to present television programmes, it fools no-one. Even those initials mark E.A.R.L. Windsor as apart from the rest – a situation from which he has struggled to escape for most of his adult life.

He is the first of the Queen's children to break away from pre-ordained royal routine and ritual, in an attempt to make his own way in life like any other citizen, despite his elevated status. But doing his own thing, always in the glare of the searchlight which relentlessly and often cruelly picks out the most famous family in the world, is a perilous path for a pioneer prince who would like to be "ordinary", as Edward has found to his cost.

He organized a highly successful, but much mocked, television event in 1987 – *It's a Royal Knockout* – which reaped more than £1.5 million for charity, and was accused of almost bringing down the monarchy. He followed family tradition and joined the armed forces, but when he decided life as a Royal Marine officer was not for him and very publicly and courageously quit, was labelled a "weeping wimp" and had his masculinity questioned. He was widely welcomed in America during a lecture tour in January 1999, but back home in Britain was accused of cashing in on his royal status.

Edward Windsor would not be human if he did not occasionally wonder if he cannot do anything right, at least in the eyes of the media. Still, he battles on, juggling royal duties with those of his day job at Ardent Productions and hopes that eventually he and his new wife will be allowed to get on with their lives and their careers, quietly and without undue attention.

child, small but healthy" and was, said one doctor, "a very serious-looking boy".

Christened on May 2, he was named after his great-great grandfather Edward VII and godfathers Lord (Tony) Snowdon, Richard, Duke of Gloucester and Prince Louis of Hesse. Soon afterwards he made his debut before the camera of society photographer Cecil Beaton in Buckingham Palace's Blue Drawing Room. As the Queen posed with her new son – "alert and curious and already a character" – Beaton felt she seemed calm, contented and happy. And her happiness was clear when, following the Trooping the Colour ceremony in June, she cradled Edward in her arms on the palace balcony for his first public appearance.

Inside, the well-rehearsed routine of bringing up royal children was in progress, with Edward in the care of his nanny in the second-floor nursery, with its grandstand view overlooking the forecourt and his mother's own soldiers keeping guard. He slept

Born with a silver spoon

That relentless spotlight, though, has been on him from the moment he was born, at Buckingham Palace in the early evening of Tuesday March 10, 1964, with the 37-year-old Queen attended by five doctors, two midwives and, at her own request, her husband – the first time Prince Philip had been present at the birth of one of his children. Himself famously born on a table at a house called "Mon Repos" on the Greek island of Corfu 43 years earlier, the always inquisitive Philip found the birth of his son an absorbing experience and has got on extremely well with his youngest child ever since.

The new baby prince, together with four-year-old Prince Andrew, completed what the Queen called her "second family", with a ten-year gap between the two younger boys and Princess Anne and Prince Charles. Edward was delivered with "no problems" and weighed in at a mere five pounds seven ounces (2.48 kilograms), "a delicate

Above: Young Edward (left) gets his first view from the balcony of Buckingham Palace, scene of many happy family occasions.

Right: An intimate moment is captured by photographer Cecil Beaton. Prince Andrew lets the new addition to family, the "delicate" Edward, take centre stage.

Above left: Edward joins cousins Sarah Armstrong-Jones and James Ogilvy (left) to learn to write two of the most important words in a child's vocabulary.

Above right: Nanny Mabel Anderson escorts seven-year-old Edward on his first day at Gibbs pre-prep school.

in the cot which had been used by his brothers and sister, played with some of their old toys and, in the old-fashioned tradition of well-to-do families, was taken to see his mother and father in the morning and before bedtime.

As the youngest, Edward was in many ways the luckiest, because the royal couple, by now well versed in running a family and The Firm, found more time to spend with him. Occasionally, the Queen liked to bath him and see him settled down for the night, with perhaps a bedtime story from his father, before they set off for evening engagements.

Educating Edward

As with their other children the Queen, ever the traditionalist in family as well as other matters, deferred to her husband on the question of Edward's education. He began his life of learning with a governess in the nursery's old schoolroom, where he was joined by two cousins – Princess Margaret's daughter, Lady Sarah Armstrong-Jones, and James Ogilvy, son of Princess Alexandra. He was, by all accounts, a very quiet boy, but also a

happy and contented one, when not being teased by his more boisterous brother Andrew.

Together, the royal cousins learned the rudiments of reading, writing and arithmetic and were often treated to afternoon outings. One they particularly loved was a visit to the BBC-TV studios to see work on the children's favourite programme, *Blue Peter*, where they were photographed cuddling uncertainly two young tiger cubs. It was a rare public glimpse of Edward. He was seldom seen or photographed, until the Queen was persuaded that an intimate film of her family – of the kind now called a fly-on-the-wall documentary – would be an excellent way of bringing the monarchy closer to the people.

For any family, to allow television cameras to eavesdrop on intimate occasions would be a major decision. For the Queen's family it was a historic one, whose effects are still discussed today. But the film, called simply *Royal Family*, was a sure-fire ratings hit, with almost 30 million viewers tuning in when it was broadcast in the summer of 1969. Not surprisingly, it was the youngest member of the cast who, Press and public agreed, stole the show.

Edward, then five, was shown playing in the snow, buying sweets, sharing a picnic with his family and, in a scene many still remember, trying bravely not to show his alarm when a string on Prince Charles's cello broke and cracked his eldest brother around the neck. Instead, Edward smiled straight at the cameras – showing, crew members

"In a velvet 'mole suit' Edward won applause from the audience"

later reported, great interest even then in professional TV men at work.

Three years later eight-year-old Edward went out into the real world when he was sent to Heatherdown preparatory school near Ascot, Berkshire. It was not too harsh a move, because he had been introduced to school life by spending days with cousin James at Gibbs, a pre-prep establishment in Kensington, London, and was by now accustomed to mixing with other boys of his own age. More importantly, his brother Andrew was also at Heatherdown, and although a four-year age gap can seem vast at that age, and Andrew kept to his own crowd, it was reassuring for Edward to see him about the place every day.

He is remembered as a quiet, dignified, self-contained boy, always anxious to do the right thing and behave properly, and he was bright and good at sport, especially cricket and rugby, and later skiing and sailing. He loved going shooting with his father at the royal homes of Sandringham in Norfolk and Balmoral in Scotland, and accompanied him to the annual Cowes Week regatta on the Isle of Wight.

Acting the part

But he will remember Heatherdown as the place where he first learned his love of the theatre – taking the lead role, at the age of 11, as the immortal Mole in *Toad of Toad Hall*, adapted from Kenneth Grahame's classic children's tale *The Wind in the Willows*. Dressed in a black velvet "mole suit" Edward won applause from the audience, including his proud and happy mother, when he burst on to the stage from a trap-door in the floor. The story of his theatrical debut is one Sophie greatly enjoys; she also loved acting as a child.

He took that love of acting with him when, at 13 years old, he left Heatherdown for Gordonstoun, the Scottish school which his father and brothers had also attended. Charles had hated the school, with its spartan remoteness and compulsory morning runs and cold showers, and said so publicly. His life there, moaned the Heir to the Throne, was "absolute hell" and he was lonely, bullied and taunted. But Edward, after an initial dislike of the establishment, soon settled down and fitted in, like Andrew before him, despite the school's harsh reputation and Charles's unpleasant experiences there.

Above: The royal wave is a vital ingredient in the life of a prince. Edward gets some early practice with mother on hand to give some useful hints on technique.

Below: Despite their 16-year age gap, Edward has always been close to the Prince of Wales. They share a love of the theatre and of daredevil sports like karting.

Above left: Looking every inch the country gentleman, Edward joins his mother and cousin Sarah Armstrong-Jones to inspect the pack of hounds at Badminton.

Above right: Edward masters the difficult art of windsurfing during Cowes Week in 1980. Sophie was to prove much less adept at this favourite summer pursuit.

"I don't think Gordonstoun's as tough as it used to be", he said later. He became a sporting all-rounder and took up squash, hockey, golf and flying, gaining his private pilot's licence by the age of 18. But again it was the theatre which really grabbed his attention and he wanted to be part of it. Among his fellow pupils was Jason Connery – son of Sean, the screen James Bond – who directed Edward in one play and said: "He never minds being told what to do. He listens hard so he can learn fast".

Edward played the character of Paris in the Gordonstoun production of Shakespeare's *Romeo and Juliet*, and before long the Queen and Prince Philip were driving over from Balmoral to see their son in Peter Shaffer's *Black Comedy* and Noël Coward's *Hay Fever*. Prince Charles even ventured to return, with future wife Lady Diana Spencer, to the scene of his "hellish" schooldays to see his youngest brother in the Feydeau farce *Hotel Paradiso*, which Edward also directed.

Away from school, Edward kept up his interest in theatre and entertainment, laying on his own plays for family and friends and even trying his hand at being a disc-jockey. To the other 25 boys who shared a dormitory with him, Edward appeared a little strait-laced and formal – having a detective with him constantly must have been at least a little intimidating – but some discovered a fine sense of humour behind that sometimes frosty facade.

Edward became head of his house and head of school, known as "Guardian", in his final year – similar honours had gone to his father and brothers – and educationally he did better than the rest of his family, gaining nine O-level exam passes (and being dubbed "Educated Ed" by the Press) before deciding to study History, English Literature, and Politics and Economics for his A-level exams.

But his work suffered because of all his extracurricular interests and his A-level results were disappointing – a grade C for English and, worse,

Ds for his other subjects. That was good enough to qualify him for entry to Cambridge University – although the fact that many more A-level students achieved much better results without gaining a place, caused a minor but very public storm when it was revealed.

Antipodean adventures

Before university, though, there was the obligatory duty for a son of the monarch to spend some time in a Commonwealth country – Charles had been to Australia and Andrew to Canada. So in September 1982, Edward set off for New Zealand to take up a post as junior master at the all-boys Collegiate School in the town of Wanganui on the North Island.

He taught third-year boys English grammar and literature, supervised their physical education sessions and cross-country runs, and joined their expeditions. He also went off on his own excursions. One was a week-long visit to Antarctica, in the footsteps of the great British explorers Sir Robert Scott and Sir Ernest Shackleton, during which he was taken by plane, helicopter, toboggan and husky-drawn sled through some of the most breathtaking scenery in the world. It was, he enthused later, "probably the most memorable week of my life".

Another highlight was when he was made an honorary member of a Maori tribe, entitling him to wear a ceremonial cloak made from kiwi feathers, which he proudly wore to welcome his brother Charles and new bride Diana during their official visit to the island.

It was a rare sartorial glimpse of Edward, who has never been particularly fussy about clothes or fashion – and in a family known for thrift had once been happy to wear hand-me-downs from his brothers. He was, however, particular about his shoes. Pupils who did odd jobs for him at the school were intrigued that the Queen's son insisted on looking after his own shoes, polishing them so diligently that you could see your face in them.

Above: The 11-year-old prince dons a gold miner's hat, while accompanying the Queen on an official visit to Canada in 1976. The trip was a good grounding for his future royal duties.

Left: Pupil turned schoolmaster, Edward's year teaching in New Zealand gave him much sought-after independence, as well as new responsibilities.

This page: Edward enjoyed Cambridge immensely, indulging a growing love of acting and the theatre. Here (above) he impresses as the judge in Arthur Miller's *The Crucible*. He also played a mean game of rugby (below), until illness and injury forced him to give up the game.

The student prince

His next change of gear came in October 1983, when Edward posed for Press photographers in his college gown on his first day as a student at Jesus College, Cambridge where, like Charles before him, he was to study Archaeology and Anthropology. After that high-profile entrance, he tried to settle down as just another student – albeit with much unwanted attention from journalists – with the usual round of lectures, tutorials, study and recreation.

He continued to play rugby and was selected to play for his college's second XV team. But he found, as Charles had done at Gordonstoun, that a prince on the playing field is somehow an irresistible target for the opposition, and after a string of injuries and a bout of glandular fever, he gave it up and concentrated on his other great love, the theatre.

Edward made his Cambridge debut playing a judge in an inter-college production of Arthur Miller's *The Crucible* and, as part of the Cambridge University Light Entertainment Society, he went on to demonstrate his versatility, playing an assortment of characters ranging from a boozer to a bumpkin. Then, when recuperation from glandular fever restricted him to taking life at a slower pace, he found his true niche behind the scenes, as stage manager and producer. Doing everything from choosing a cast to painting scenery and selling tickets, he said he "really enjoyed putting these things together and trying to turn what was an idea into a reality".

There was nothing real, though, about a widely-published picture of Edward roped to railway tracks in front of a thundering locomotive, a stunt designed to publicize one show. It made the production a sell-out and the Queen and her sister Margaret were sitting amongst the appreciative audience. But all too soon his theatrical days were over and, after allowing extracurricular activities to interfere with his studies once again, he left Cambridge with a "perfectly respectable" but average class 2.ii degree.

Looking back during an interview with a Cambridge newspaper, the student prince revealed: "These have been three of the best years of my life. Everybody says that about school, but I don't think I ever enjoyed school as much as I enjoyed university. There's a wonderful mix of people, and I am never likely to mix so informally with such a wide range of people". That was certainly true.

Ahead lay time with an entirely different group of people who could also play hard, but whose regime would be a test for anyone, and the Royal Marine Commandos would present Edward with the most difficult decision of his life.

When the going gets tough ...

Edward had wanted to become a Royal Marine since he was a boy, and joining them would be a suitable and traditional career route for a young royal. His father is Captain General of the Marines and both his brothers were in the armed forces, with Andrew flying a Sea King helicopter during the Falklands War in 1982. Accordingly, in September 1982, Edward became a Second Lieutenant at the Commando Training Centre in Lympstone, Devon, and the following year spent a week on detachment in Belize with 40 Commando Royal Marines.

With jungle training and trekking, river patrols and living in the rawest of conditions, it was a tough test for any young man, which Edward

"He found his true niche behind the scenes, as stage manager and producer"

survived. He wore his Marines uniform proudly for the first time in public in November 1983, when the Queen unveiled a memorial statue of Earl Mountbatten, Edward's great-uncle, who was assassinated in 1979. He had been Colonel Commandant of the Marines.

The royal recruit turned up at Lympstone to embark upon his full-time training in earnest in September 1986 and, refuting suggestions that he'd receive special treatment in earning the Marines' prized green beret, his commanding officer said: "It will not be handed to Edward on a plate. He will have to earn it". Although he was treated exactly like the other 36 officer-material recruits who joined with him, and earned the same unprincely salary of £7,391 a year, there was no way that Edward would ever fit in with the rest of them.

Wherever they went, one recruit said later, a vehicle with two Special Branch police officers would follow half a mile behind, shadowing the prince's activities. When they all went drinking

Below: As any mother would, the Queen proudly greets her son in his Royal Marines uniform at RAF Benson. She had no idea at this stage of her son's unhappiness with the military career mapped out for him.

BEFORE HE MET HER

The girls in Edward's life

For a young man whose masculinity has been called into question – not least when he was unfairly accused of "wimping out" of the Marines – Prince Edward has had more than his fair share of bright, attractive girls who have been only too pleased to appear on the arm of the Queen's youngest son. Some have been real friendships, but others have been hyped by the Press, keen to build up an image of a "playboy prince" just as they had with his brothers. But while Andrew and Charles were happy to play along with this image, Edward was certainly not.

"My anonymity has gone and I accept that", he said, aged 22, "but you become very conscious of the feeling that if you try to get to know anybody they are going to suffer a stigma for the rest of their lives. I cannot have a normal relationship with just about anybody, but that's just the way it goes". Some did not mind suffering the "stigma", including a Balmoral housemaid who is supposed to have introduced Edward to the joys of love-making. According to a fellow servant, she waltzed into the staff dining room and told everyone she had just been his "first". To the shy prince, the knowledge that his love life was all round the castle was a painful lesson.

Edward's first real girlfriend was a lovely, ordinary girl called Shelley Whitborn who had caught Edward's eye while he was at Gordonstoun. She had touched the young prince's heart when she nursed his pony, Flash, back to health, and they enjoyed numerous dates. It was also an early indication that he would not necessarily be seeking female companions from amongst the aristocracy.

A princely conquest

While in New Zealand Edward was a popular escort and "certainly not shy with girls" according to local girl Alison Bell. On his return, he fell for Romy Adlington, a beautiful 17-year-old model who he met at Cowes, always a happy hunting ground for Edward. He pursued Romy keenly and eventually persuaded her to join him for supper at Buckingham Palace. Supper turned into early morning tea, brought to them in bed by Edward's valet. Romy recalled, "Edward looked at me with what I can only describe as amused conquest, I think he felt quite proud that he could have a girlfriend to stay the night with him, right under his mother's nose. The Queen was in residence but I don't think she would have liked to know I was tucked up in bed with her youngest son."

Romy later revealed how she was accepted by the family. "The Queen was immediately friendly and charming", she observed. But Romy's busy modelling schedule and Edward's studies and royal duties made it impossible for the couple's relationship and their affair petered out.

Back at Cambridge, Edward had a series of dates, sometimes "kicking out" his long-suffering detective from his rooms while he entertained. One of them, Eleanor Weightman, became a long-standing friend. She was a multilingual, sports-loving history student whose diminuitive stature earned her the pet name of Munchkin. Although they laughed a lot and enjoyed each other's company, the spark of romance was always missing.

Another girl he became close to was Georgia May, a 22-year-old financial adviser. She was heavily tipped in the media to be Edward's bride, but she found the scrutiny of the Press impossible. She admitted, "All this attention is terrifying me".

Privately, Edward told friends he would not wish being his girlfriend on his worst enemy. He would resort to throwing smoke screens for the benefit of the Press. Escorts like TV presenter Ulrika Jonsson received plenty of media attention, but did not figure much in the prince's life. He was more interested in Cambridge student Rhian-Anwen Roberts, a bright and discreet girl who remains one of his closest friends.

Opposite, main picture: Edward, always the gentlemanly escort, has never aspired to the "playboy prince" label.

Opposite, inset: Romy Adlington, showing the cool model looks that captivated the young prince.

Below: The vivacious musical star Ruthie Henshall remains a good friend.

Above: Edward found Georgia May great fun, but she couldn't cope with the media attention their romance brought.

Before he met Sophie, the last girl linked with Edward was the West End star Ruthie Henshall. Edward missed her first night in *Crazy For You* because he didn't want to steal her thunder, a typically thoughtful gesture. Instead, he joined friends celebrating Rhian-Anwen's birthday. Like many of the women in his life, Ruthie has remained on very good terms with Edward who she describes as a "jolly nice guy". When she fell in love with fellow actor John Gordon Sinclair, her mother Gloria said of Edward: "He woke her up to the fact that nice men are much nicer to be with and I thank him for that."

To stay on and tough it out would be the easy way, but to quit now would bring an avalanche of negative publicity. His parents urged him to complete the training course, but agreed to respect his final decision on the matter. However, his former Cambridge tutor, Dr Gavin Mackenzie, wanted him to quit. "I could not teach Edward anything about physical courage or moral integrity", he said. "It might take a bit more of both qualities to resign than to remain".

"Breaking with tradition Edward had shown great courage"

By the end of the Christmas period, Edward had decided to leave the Marines, but agreed to travel to Lympstone before he made the final break. Before he could do so, news of his unhappiness leaked to the Press – and although many trainees get "the wobbles" and want to quit in the early days, Edward was harshly singled out, with claims that he found the training too tough and wept for days as he wrestled with his problem. "The Weeping Wimp of Windsor" was how one American newspaper unsympathetically described his plight.

A few days later Buckingham Palace announced that Edward was "leaving the Marines with great

Above: The training regime for a young recruit was exceptionally hard, but Edward did not shirk his responsibilities until he had made up his mind that his future lay elsewhere.

Right: Despite concerns that Prince Philip would be angry or hurt at Edward's decision to leave the Marines, he showed sympathy and understanding to the son who has always been his favourite.

together in nearby Topsham – seen as an essential part of the Commando bonding process – the atmosphere was strained and Edward, never a drinker and dubbed "The Apple Juice Kid", seemed ill at ease: "He had problems in terms of mingling", said the recruit. "People were just not sure, and he didn't muck in".

A farewell to arms

Both the prince and the Marines wanted it to work, and Edward even stoically accepted the apparently ritual custom of having mud rammed in his ears, mouth, nose and shirt by his comrades, when he turned up to watch a rugby match. "Just a skylark" was the official explanation, and Edward never complained. But when he'd served just 12 weeks, and went home to Sandringham for a family Christmas, he was agonizing over whether another five years in the Marines was what he really wanted.

regret, but has decided that he does not want to make the service his long-time career". And as the public debate rumbled on, the much-maligned Marine walked to church with his father by his side – a signal that Philip was wholeheartedly behind his son's decision.

In time, many came to agree that in breaking with tradition and choosing his own way of life, Edward had shown great courage. One fellow recruit says: "I respect him for saying 'This is not for me'. That takes as much courage as staying in". British journalist Robin Eggar, who spent 15 months living with the Marines for his book *Commando: Survival of the Fittest*, believes the presence of the royal bodyguards "simply reinforced the natural barrier between prince and paupers. The sad thing for the prince is he really never had a chance".

And Edward? "I was never going to fit in as I had envisaged, and that, more than anything else, decided me", he told biographer Ingrid Seward, who records how Edward took his leave of Lympstone and "that night, for the first and only time in his life, he got roaring drunk".

Right: As a Commando, Edward looked like the real thing – and was fulfilling a boyhood dream – but the burden of regimental life proved too much. After only three months of full-time training, the prince resigned his commission.

Chapter Four

THE GIRL FROM HOMESTEAD FARMHOUSE

An accomplished young woman, ready to forge ahead in both her career and private life

———————◆———————

S ophie Rhys-Jones enjoyed an idyllic childhood in the sleepy Kent village of Brenchley, 60 miles south-east of London. Her family, friends and teachers remember her as smiling, cheerful and enthusiastic in everything she did, whether fighting for victory in the netball team or acting in the school play.

She has never lost her natural optimism and energy. When she moved to London as a 19-year-old, she worked hard and played hard. Like Prince Edward, she was happy to start off sorting mail and making tea in an office job before moving on to better things.

But unlike the prince, she was free to opt out for a year. She took a holiday job in Switzerland for the winter season, fell madly in love with a handsome ski instructor and accompanied him back to Australia. Although the relationship did not last, Sophie made the best of the situation and spent the rest of the year travelling around the country.

By the time she returned to London, the new Sophie was an accomplished and worldly young woman, ready to forge ahead in both her career and private life.

Left: Sophie enjoys a weekend break in Dartmouth, Devon, with a group of girlfriends. She has always been a sociable young woman, who also inspires great loyalty in her friends.

"Young Sophie loved it there and neighbours remember just how happy she was"

Sophie Rhys-Jones had her first experience of life at a royal court when she was very young – and fitted in so well that, as the Queen would say later of her new daughter-in-law: "You wouldn't notice her in a crowd". She *was* part of a crowd, one of many girls cast as Saxons at the court of King Ethelbert in a school play. "And I'm afraid", smiles her former headmaster Robin Peverett, "the poor girl didn't have even a small speaking part, although she may have muttered an occasional 'Rhubarb! Rhubarb!' along with the rest of them".

The family pedigree

It was the nearest Sophie, then 11, would come to being part of a royal family until she met Edward. Since then, though, research has discovered that her own family is not without its royal connections. Her mother, Mary O'Sullivan, is descended from humble Irish stock in the West Cork town of Bantry, which still boasts many O'Sullivans, a beautiful bay and a statue of St Brendan the Navigator (who some say discovered America). But until now it has had just two royal links – paintings of King George III and Queen Charlotte on show at Bantry House, which were presented by the King to the first Earl of Bantry, who helped repel a French invasion force in 1796.

Sophie's father, Christopher, has a more impressive pedigree. He is descended from a long line of Welsh warriors and, through his father's 1928 marriage to Patricia Molesworth – a descendant of the 17th-century diplomat the first

Viscount Molesworth – has links with the Stua[rt] kings, the Queen Mother and the late Dian[a,] Princess of Wales. And it was that Moleswor[th] connection which intrigued journalist Nig[el] Dempster when he was a boarder at St Peter['s] Preparatory School in Lympstone, the Devon tow[n] where Prince Edward would later train, for a whil[e] with the Marines.

Grandpa's school

Dempster recalls: "Christopher's father Theo, wh[o] we called Rhys, was the proprietor and headmaste[r] and while I was there the name Nigel Moleswor[th] became very well-known because of a book (*Dow[n] with Skool!*, featuring that subversive schoolboy[)] and Rhys's wife admitted *she* was a Moleswort[h] too. Around 1953, his sons Theo and Chris came [to] work as teachers, filling in until they got on wit[h] their careers. He also had a lovely daughter calle[d] Helen, whose passion was horses. She rode almo[st] every day on Woodbury Common, where th[e] Marines trained". One day, though, her horse di[ed]

Right: Mr and Mrs Rhys-Jones greet the Press outside Homestead Farmhouse after their daughter's engagement is announced. They have always been supportive of Sophie, despite the daunting prospect of having a royal son-in-law.

Above: The picturesque village of Brenchley, complete with a traditional Kentish oast house. Sophie spent a happy, carefree childhood in this peaceful rural setting.

not return. "Helen had been thrown and killed. She was only 24, and it was a very sad day for everyone at the school. But it's nice that she is remembered in Sophie's second name, Helen, after the aunt she never knew".

Life at Homestead Farmhouse

In 1955, Sophie's father left his teaching post at the school and began an engineering career in Birmingham, which later entailed travelling around the world. He also met and married Mary O'Sullivan, the daughter of a bank inspector, who worked as a London secretary and, with a flat near Sloane Square, qualified as an early "Sloane Ranger" who once met Prince Philip on a yacht at Cowes on the Isle of Wight.

Mr and Mrs Rhys-Jones made their first home in the Buckinghamshire village of Ickford and started their family – first David and two years later Sophie Helen. She was born at the Nuffield Maternity Home in Oxford on January 20, 1965 and her first name was chosen by chance, because when she was pregnant, Mary overheard another mother call out "Sophie!" to her little girl and decided she liked the name. Soon afterwards the family moved to Kent, to be near the ports of Dover and Folkestone for Chris's frequent business trips to mainland Europe. They settled in the beautiful village of Brenchley, near Tunbridge Wells, where their first home was a small house close to the village centre. Then, after a few years, they found their dream – Homestead Farmhouse – and they haven't moved since.

It's a cosy and comfortable 18th-century farmhouse, hidden from view at the end of a quiet lane on the edge of the village, with four bedrooms overlooking the peaceful Kent countryside, and a perfect place to bring up a family. Young Sophie loved it there – and still goes back home whenever her hectic schedule permits – and neighbours remember just how happy she was. Doors were always open in the friendly rural community,

Above: An outgoing and popular girl, Sophie was always the centre of attention during her school days. Here (centre, in orange T-shirt) she larks about with school chums at Kent College for Girls.

"and Sophie and her brother often used to come in and chat", one neighbour remembers. "They were very nice children and we were always pleased to see them". As her fifth birthday approached, Sophie joined brother David at Dulwich College Preparatory School in Cranbrook, some 10 miles (16 kilometres) from Brenchley, where the fees could put a strain on a young family's finances. But Mary Rhys-Jones, who worked for an estate agent in nearby Paddock Wood, used her secretarial skills and took on spare-time typing work to make sure her children's schooling was the best. And it was.

Halcyon days

Sophie still looks back on her days at the school as close to idyllic, with what seemed like a huge field to play in, a swimming pool, tree houses and a play house in which, one of her friends from those days has recalled, they once locked themselves in and refused to come out. When the idea caught on, and play house rebellions escalated, the school solved the problem by simply taking off the door. Later there were ballet and riding lessons and, as she moved up through the school, the serious business of academic work, but it was, to all intents and purposes, a country school

education many would envy. "Some people get us mixed up with *the* Dulwich College", says Robin Peverett, head of the Cranbrook prep school for 20 years, "and they assume that Sophie went there and was a sophisticated City girl even then. But that is far from the truth. *Our* Dulwich College was a far, far different place, very rural and absolutely beautiful, with apple orchards and oast houses – I lived in one with my family – and I'd say a perfect place to go to school".

Sophie certainly thought so. "In 20 years I knew vast numbers of pupils", adds Mr Peverett, "but I very clearly remember Sophie Rhys-Jones and her brother David. We believed that to get the most out of pupils they should thoroughly enjoy the school and be absolutely relaxed and happy, and Sophie always seemed to love us – and indeed still says so. She was very natural, very easy to get on with and very popular. She was cheerful, a good games player and did her work well – just the sort of pupil we liked to have and who clearly liked us".

It's the sort of school report to make any parent immensely proud, and ample reward for Mary Rhys-Jones' extra hours slaving over her typewriter, but Robin Peverett says Sophie deserved it: "She did well and didn't put on airs or try to be fancy, which would not have gone down too well. She was just a jolly nice girl who fitted very easily into the school and threw herself into everything with great enthusiasm". Like Prince Edward at his prep school, Sophie loved acting and getting involved in drama productions, and her former headmaster particularly remembers that first appearance she made at a royal court, in a play about St Augustine.

"It was called *Case 34 – Augustine* and was very dramatic stuff written by an extremely famous playwright – me!" laughs Robin Peverett. "I always wrote the plays because I had to include huge casts and masses of girls – about 70 leavers – and that year Sophie was among them. She was in a crowd of Saxon girls at the court of Ethelbert and it was far from a star part, but they all did it very well. We took over a local church and all traipsed down there to put it on and it was quite exciting.

"She knew how to get on well with people and to be herself, and be happy"

"Sophie left us in 1976, when she passed her exams for Kent College, but I know she still remembers her days with us very fondly. I wrote to congratulate her when her engagement was announced, and I had a very nice letter back with a postscript saying 'I so loved my time at DCPS'. That's exactly what we wanted, because if pupils are happy and enjoy themselves they learn well". And Sophie's well-earned lessons and strong and sensible character, he predicts, will stand her in good stead for her new role as a member of the royal family: "The two things that come across over all those years is that she was such a happy girl with what I rate pretty highly – common sense. She knew how to get on well with people and to be herself, and be happy with her own persona. That made it easy for her to get on at school, and easy for us who were trying to teach her, and I'm sure she'll do well in the future, too".

A good sport

The next step for Sophie, however, was to go as a day girl to Kent College for Girls in Pembury, where she is again remembered as a bright, happy and enthusiastic pupil, still keen on theatre, ballet, riding – and sport. She loved gymnastics, hockey and especially netball, and a picture of her in the under-12s team, taken in the Queen's Silver Jubilee Year of 1977, has gone around the world and brought fleeting fame to the team-mates seen with her. One, then Jane Jones and now Mrs Jane O'Neill, says: "That picture seems to be printed everywhere. It's a shame it wasn't taken at a party, or when we were looking more presentable". Another, Mrs Tina (née Gooder) Evans, clears up a minor mystery: "Sophie was the team's reserve, and that's why she's not wearing a

red bib like the rest of us. But all I remember about the picture being taken is that it was very cold!"

All, though, recall Sophie Rhys-Jones as a lovely, sports-loving girl who always did her best. She left school at 16 with a "respectable" eight O-level examination passes and was keen to embark on a career and start forging her way in the world. To further her ambitions, she enrolled in 1981 at West Kent College in Tonbridge for a two-year Professional Secretarial Course, studying typing, shorthand, business structure and office administration, and for A-level examinations in English Literature and Law. Lecturer Marion Vellino, who taught her, remembers "a popular, lively and bubbly girl". "Like all teenagers", she adds, "Sophie could grumble about getting up on a Monday morning when, like her contemporaries, she enjoyed discussing the weekend's activities". Years later, Mrs Vellino would say: "Sophie seems very aware of the responsibilities she is taking on in marrying Prince Edward. I am sure she will make a wonderful wife".

Above: Eleven-year-old Sophie (far left) poses with her netball team-mates. She continues to love sporting activities, and now includes snowboarding, horseriding and real tennis among her favourite pursuits.

Left: Kent College, the £1,400-a-term school where Sophie spent most of her formative teenage years.

SOPHIE'S SUITORS

Past romances and the lovers who remain her friends

Below: Attractive and fun-loving, Sophie's charms have always made her popular with the opposite sex. One former lover said: "I will always have a place in my heart for her".

Like Prince Edward, Sophie Rhys-Jones was seldom without an attractive partner before they found each other – and all of them stay the best of friends with her. "Sophie has always been fun to be with", one ex-boyfriend says, "but she's very sensible too, and the fact that she's stayed friends with us shows what a mature attitude she has".

Sophie's first serious boyfriend was dark-haired and handsome David Kinder. They were both 15, and met at a theatre workshop held in Tonbridge School. Their schooldays' romance lasted only a matter of months, but David, who went on to become an actor (with one role in the *Doctor Who* TV series) before turning to teaching, is still a friend of that "lovely girl" he fell for all those years ago. "Prince Edward is a very lucky man", he said when their engagement was announced.

At 17, Sophie went out with sports-loving John Blackman, who introduced her to the joys of skiing and, when she first left home for London, arranged for her to stay at his parents' South Kensington home until she found a place of her own. John, who later built up a successful computer software company, remains one of her closest male friends.

There were other brief romances, including family friend Rupert Keane – to whom Mr Rhys-Jones is godfather and who was at one time considered to be a potential son-in-law by Sophie's hopeful parents – and insurance broker Robert Scott-Mackie, whom Sophie met while she was doing her college secretarial course. "She was vivacious, good looking and had a particularly nice figure", he reflects fondly. "Unfortunately, we only went out together briefly".

When she joined Capital Radio, the bubbly promotions girl was a much sought-after companion, and for a while dated sports journalist Andrew Parkinson, son of TV chat show host Michael. "We went out a few times and had a bit of fun", he has said. "But that was all. We were never serious".

More serious was her year-long romance with an "older man". Businessman Jeremy Barkley, known as "Jez", was 11 years her senior, and sold Sophie her first car – "a wonderful 1967 Morris Minor", she said later. It was to be her longest relationship before she met Prince Edward. Then she left England behind for her ski rep job in Switzerland, and that ill-fated "holiday romance" with Australian ski instructor Michael O'Neill.

Back in Britain, Sophie found fun and excitement with dentist Tom King, who had a London practice in Chelsea and spent all his spare time flying a private plane. Together they enjoyed frequent trips across the English

Channel to Le Touquet in France, skiing weekends – and sometimes bumpy landings. That romance cooled, too, after a time, but he and Sophie stay friends. In fact, Sophie can look back on all her bachelor-girl romances with very happy memories. Except, perhaps, for one.

It started at a party arranged by air stewardess Ulrike von Herwath, who had invited Sophie to share her London flat on her return from Australia. She also asked Sophie to a weekend party, with an invitation promising "cosmic croquet, visual vibes, mellow munchies, dizzy juggling, BBQ, dancing, tennis and swimming" over three days at Ulrike's parents' home in Benenden, Kent, in the summer of 1992.

At the party, Ulrike introduced Sophie to a German friend called Jan Heissenberg and they linked up to play tennis and swim in the open-air pool. Later Heissenberg, now 36 and living in Frankfurt, told a newspaper they had also danced, kissed and eventually fallen asleep in each other's arms. Later still, just three months before her wedding, another paper claimed Heissenberg had pictures of a topless Sophie beside the pool and was prepared to sell them for publication.

Aside from this one fling which led to kiss-and-tell revelations in newspapers, Sophie has always enjoyed great loyalty and enduring friendships with her former boyfriends, who all speak very highly of her. And it was these qualities which were to play an essential role in the lasting success of Sophie's romance with Edward.

Opposite, top: Sophie's first boyfriend, David Kinder, still remains a close friend.

Opposite, bottom: During her radio days, Sophie enjoyed dates with Andrew Parkinson.

Right: Jan Heissenberg, the only man to kiss-and-tell about his brief fling with Sophie.

Below: Despite spending a year as a single girl in Australia, Sophie wasn't without her admirers.

Right: Seventeen-year-old Sophie gets into the party spirit at brother David's 21st birthday at a local pub. A natural extrovert, she's always known how to let her hair down and have fun.

Below: The Halfway House, the country watering hole where Sophie earned money waitressing as a student, is now a mecca for TV crews from around the world, looking for Sophie's story.

Meanwhile, her "bubbly" charm helped her get a part-time job as a waitress at The Halfway House, a 300-year-old pub near her Brenchley home. "She worked here for about six months while she was at college", says Robin Pratt, the current proprietor of the typically English country pub, "and though I wasn't here then, locals tell me she was always cheery and attentive".

Since her engagement was announced, The Halfway House has seen nothing of its former waitress, except on television and in newspapers. "She was in Brenchley at Christmas, not long before the engagement was announced", reveals Robin Pratt, "and she went to midnight Mass, but of course it must be difficult for her to pop in here now. But her parents, very nice, friendly people, come fairly regularly for lunch or dinner, and Sophie's link with us means we've had TV crews here from all over the world – America, Australia, Germany. She's helped put the place on the map, and we'll certainly be celebrating her wedding. Not a street party, like they have in the East End of London – we're a little more refined and restrained around here – but at the very least we'll raise a glass or two to toast her happiness".

> ## *"She hasn't really changed. With Sophie it's a case of what you see is what you get"*

Bright lights, big city

With good results from college, Sophie set out to start on the career ladder, and in 1983 her credentials quickly landed her a position as secretary with the Quentin Bell Organisation, then a fledgling PR company with a couple of offices in Portman Square, London. "It was her first real job", recalls Managing Director Trevor Morris from the Covent Garden headquarters of QBO, "and I think that even then she'd decided she wanted to do something in our line of work. We were just about four people then and everybody mucked in, with Sophie looking after all of us, doing everything from typing letters and sorting the mail to making the tea.

"She was a real presence around the office, very bright and bubbly and with no airs or graces, just very lively and efficient. I met her again a few years ago, and she hasn't really changed. With Sophie it's a case of 'what you see is what you get', and we certainly got a very bright secretary. She got a basic grounding with us, learned as she went along, and then moved on".

By now Sophie was well in tune with life in London, sharing a flat in West Kensington with a friend, finding no shortage of attractive suitors, making new friends, but popping home to Brenchley to keep up with her old ones at weekends. For a young, attractive, single girl it was an exciting time, and more came when, in 1986, she landed a new job in the Press office of Capital Radio, London's leading music station. After a while, she was also helping in the busy promotions department which was run by Anita Hamilton, who would later play an indirect role in her meeting with Edward.

"It was rumoured pictures existed of Sophie and Tarrant which might embarrass her"

Meanwhile, her job brought her into daily contact with famous stars, like Rolling Stone Mick Jagger, who dropped in for interviews, and the station's often zany disc-jockeys. Among them was Chris Tarrant – now said to earn £1.1 million a year as one of Britain's top DJs and much more as a popular TV presenter – and they formed an enduring friendship which, years later, was to cause a huge storm, upset Sophie and infuriate Tarrant.

Caught on camera

When she became "Edward's girl", it was rumoured that pictures existed of Sophie and Tarrant which might embarrass her if they were published. Among them was one taken by Tarrant's former radio co-host, Kara Noble, during a Capital trip to Spain in 1988. It showed the couple in the back of a car, with Tarrant playfully lifting Sophie's bikini top to expose a breast. Among the first to hear the rumours was Brian MacLaurin, a close friend of both Sophie and Tarrant, who himself once worked in radio and still has many contacts in the industry. He knew the pictures were totally innocuous – "the sort many young people have taken when

they're out partying, or on holiday with friends" – but realized that Noble might be pressured into selling them to the newspapers, which could put a different interpretation on them.

So MacLaurin's next move was to approach Noble's recent employers, London radio station Heart FM, and suggest she relinquish her copyright of the photos for a donation to a charity of her choice. The copyright could then be handed to Sophie – and the pictures probably destroyed. But it was Sophie herself, believing Noble's word that she would never sell the photographs, who vetoed the deal. "Sophie was prepared to trust Kara's word on that", MacLaurin said, "but history has since told us it was the wrong decision". Noble did sell the the pictures, for a reported £100,000 – and just three weeks before the wedding, the tabloid newspaper *The Sun* devoted five pages to a "world picture exclusive" with shots which, it claimed, "show an amazing intimacy between the pair".

It sparked widespread outrage. The Palace condemned the newspaper for "premeditated cruelty" against Sophie and lodged a formal protest with the Press Complaints Commission. *The Sun* issued a grovelling apology and halted its series.

Above: Sophie's London flat in Vereker Road, West Kensington, which was later to be the scene of secret rendezvous with the prince.

Above left: Popular DJ and TV presenter Chris Tarrant, who Sophie worked with at Capital Radio, has continued to be a good friend through the years.

Kara Noble was sacked from her job at Heart FM, and on his own radio show, Tarrant angrily attacked her "betrayal". He told listeners: "Sophie is, and was, a great laugh. Really good fun. A great extrovert. Full stop! She was always a totally moral, really decent girl. Nothing immoral happened between us, before or after this picture".

Edward, who Sophie had told about the pictures at the start of their romance, was said to be "very angry", and Sophie was feeling "shattered and betrayed". But, through Brian MacLaurin, she said she wanted that to be an end to the matter. "Prince Edward and Sophie are obviously very upset that Kara did this", he said, "but they want to move on and look to the future. Sophie doesn't want to harbour a grudge".

Love in a cold climate

When those pictures were taken, Sophie was still a carefree, fun-loving girl enjoying life and London, but after three years at Capital she decided to spread her wings – and found the ideal opportunity to do so by combining the necessity of earning a living with her great love of skiing. She applied for a job as a ski rep with the Bladon Lines travel company, who sent her to the Swiss resort of Crans-Montana for four months. It was hard work with long hours, organizing the chalet girls and arranging après-ski activities for groups of guests, for little more than £60 a week. Even so, the food and accommodation were free, and she could ski every day. Sophie loved every minute of it – especially when, in a holiday scenario which could grace the pages of a romantic novel, she fell head over heels for her ski instructor, a tall and handsome young Australian called Michael O'Neill.

They shared every moment they could grab together, skiing, skating, bobsleighing, snowboarding (at which Sophie showed off her skills on

Opposite: Tall, dark and handsome, Australian ski instructor Michael O'Neill swept Sophie off her feet during a working holiday in Crans-Montana, Switzerland, and she swapped the snowy peaks of the Alps for the beaches of Sydney.

Above right: Out on the piste, Sophie (far right) enjoys work and play in equal measures with her fellow ski reps.

Below right: After the chalet guests went off for the day, Sophie (right) and her friends were free to go skiing, skating, snowboarding – or even enjoy a snowball fight.

her first post-engagement holiday with Edward), dining out with friends or just being alone. And when the winter season ended and Michael suggested she go home with him to Sydney, Australia, the normally level-headed and sensible 25-year-old thought something like "What the hell!" and went. But, like many impulsive holiday romances, it did not last. For reasons neither of them has ever revealed, even to close friends, the couple parted and went their separate ways. Alone at the opposite side of the world, with no job or flat to return home to, Sophie decided to make the most of the situation and made up her mind to spend a year Down Under.

Sharing a flat with a friend from London, she quickly found herself work with a Sydney air-freight firm, where her secretarial skills and good-natured efficiency were as appreciated as they had been back at home. She prepared invoices, booked

couriers, chased packages and, says Jonathan Miller, the man who employed her, "didn't really mind what she did, including making the coffee. But really I think Sophie just wanted to let her hair down and have a good time". Another friend in Australia adds: "Sophie has a personality that people here can relate to. She's a get-up-and-go girl who doesn't sit back in a prim and proper English manner. The great thing about her is that she is a very strong person who doesn't let things get to her".

Out of work hours she got together with new-found friends for beach parties and barbecues, sailing trips and sightseeing. She joined a deep-sea diving club and became a great enthusiast for her new sport. Then, after ten months, Sophie decided to see more of Australia's breathtaking scenery. After linking up with another British girl, she travelled to Queensland, went diving around the

Great Barrier Reef, and in Cairns, the port on Trinity Bay, tried her hand at another adventurous sport – bungee jumping. She loved it all.

But, in June 1991, Sophie decided it was time to return to Britain and get on with her career. Though she could never have guessed it, a far greater adventure lay ahead.

Opposite: A tanned and relaxed stowaway, Sophie curls up with a bottle of beer in her cabin bunk-bed. A year in Australia gave her the chance to broaden her horizons.

Right: Dancing the night away, Sophie (centre) enjoys the nightlife while in Australia. Weekends usually revolved around a whirlwind of parties and sporting activities.

Below: Sophie (far right) joins friends for a weekend trip on the luxury yacht *Meridian*, sailing around the secluded bays that dot the coast of south-eastern Australia.

Chapter Five

A CHANCE MEETING

A brief encounter at Queen's Club changes Sophie's destiny

They met purely by chance – because a tough TV executive refused to allow former tennis star Sue Barker to pose with Prince Edward for a charity event. Instead, Sophie's boss took his pretty employee as a last-minute stand-in, and the scene was set for romance. There was no sudden spark at that first meeting, but Sophie leaned on Edward's shoulder as she posed with him, with no awe on her part and no objection from him.

The courtship that followed had all the ingredients of a romantic thriller: clandestine meetings, a crazy car chase through London, assumed names and a secret rendezvous in a quiet suburban home. They managed to keep their deepening friendship to themselves for almost three months, with quiet dates and stolen moments, as Sophie entered a new and totally different world, met the Queen and her family, and realized that her life could soon change completely. And forever.

That day came sooner than she had expected, when a famous reporter, Andrew Morton, evaded tight security at her office, walked straight up to her desk and said: "Sophie Rhys-Jones, can I be the first person to call you Your Royal Highness?" From then on, the girl from Homestead Farmhouse would be under the constant scrutiny of the media, because of her association with the most famous family in Britain.

Left: Edward and Sophie step out together at the Royal Yacht Squadron Ball at Cowes in 1994. In the past, Edward had first met some of his previous girlfriends at this annual sailing event, but now, after a year together, he proudly escorted the new love of his life, Sophie.

"Prince Edward was happy to do the pictures with Sophie"

That great adventure, Sophie's chance meeting with Prince Edward, came after she returned from Australia in the summer of 1991. The enthusiastic 26-year-old soon found a job in which her expertise helped promote the work of the London-based Macmillan Cancer Relief charity. However, after a year working at the charity, she decided to look for something new, and was recruited by Brian MacLaurin, the thrusting boss of a new public relations company called MacLaurin Communications.

He remembers: "Sophie and I have a mutual friend in Anita Hamilton, who I worked with when I was Communications Director of LBC (the London commercial radio station). About a year after I set up this company, Anita said: 'If you are looking for staff, I know a very bright girl who worked for me at Capital and would be perfect. Would you see her?' I agreed, and Sophie came to our offices.

"I wouldn't say she stood out in a crowd, but in this business I always look for fire in the eyes, enthusiasm and energy, and someone who is fun and vivacious, and would relate to clients. Sophie had all those attributes. She was lively, intelligent, well-read and had a good grasp of current affairs, which is crucial, and was very good with people. At the end of our interview, I hired her as an account executive, on around £20,000 a year".

In her early days with the company, Sophie was delighted to be working again with Chris Tarrant, one of its clients – "they'd met at Capital, so it was a natural link" – and later helped with TV-presenter Noel Edmonds, then hosting his TV *House Party*. But, contrary to a story which is still trotted out, she was never a spokesperson for the unspeakable

Right: The prince's love affair with real tennis began after he had to give up rugby at university. The historically royal game was the perfect setting for his on-court courtship with Sophie.

"Mr Blobby", the pink-and-spotted character who regularly wreaked havoc on Edmonds' shows. Although the Press later delighted in making a great play of their supposed association ("Edward falls for Blobby's girl"), their link was minimal.

A much more interesting encounter, however, was not far away. MacLaurin explains: "The then head of the Radio Authority, a delightful man called Peter Baldwin, wanted to launch a major charitable event on commercial radio, with all the stations raising money. He spoke about it to Simon Cole of Unique Broadcasting, an independent production company, who advised him to get in a good PR firm. That's where I came in".

The prince and the PR girl

Prince Edward was involved in the charity event because money raised went to the Duke of Edinburgh Award scheme, and he, Baldwin, Cole and MacLaurin met to discuss the possibilities. One idea was for Edward to play a game of real tennis, one of his abiding passions, to raise money, but MacLaurin suggested there would be added interest if he took part in a challenge, playing for as long as he possibly could. The idea took some flak as it was floated through the mysterious waters of Palace protocol, but after a lot of hassles it was finally cleared. To publicize the event, MacLaurin proposed a photo-call with Edward at London's exclusive Queen's Club, where the world's leading

tennis stars play every summer before the Wimbledon tennis tournament. And to add a touch of feminine glamour, it was arranged that the prince would be photographed with Sue Barker, Britain's former number one and world number three tennis player, who was building a successful career as a sports broadcaster.

"The idea", says Brian MacLaurin, "was that Sue would wear a succession of sweatshirts with the logos of all the radio stations involved, ensuring us maximum publicity throughout the UK. But on the morning of the shoot, I got a telephone call from David Hill, then the Head of Sport for Sky TV. He said: 'What are you trying to do with my girl Sue Barker? Unless she is wearing exclusively Sky branding, you cannot use Sue Barker!' I said: 'Don't be ridiculous! This is a charity thing …', but he just said: 'Not interested!' and put the phone down on me!".

The cool MacLaurin was facing a minor crisis: "The photo-shoot was arranged and Prince Edward was almost on his way – and there was no-one to do the pictures with him. But there, sitting in my office, was this bright and pretty young girl, and I suddenly thought that she might be the one to save the day. My idea was to take Sophie with me, see whether Prince Edward was happy to do the pictures with her, and take it from there. But Sophie was quite nervous when I put the idea to her. She said something like: 'Oh, my goodness! I don't think …', and if I'd given her more time she'd probably have tried everything to get out of it.

"But I said: 'Come on, it's no problem!' and got her out of the door and on the way". Was it a request, or an order? "It was an instruction", laughs Brian MacLaurin. "My staff know me very well. I'm a little bit of an autocrat, and I only ever instruct! So there was no question of her not doing it".

Above: The now-famous first picture of Edward and Sophie, taken in August 1993. Although it was a promotional shot, since then they have rarely been pictured looking so relaxed and natural in each other's company.

That fateful day in the late summer of 1993, MacLaurin drove Sophie the short distance from his plush new offices in Berghem Mews, Hammersmith, to Queen's Club "and waited rather nervously for Prince Edward to arrive. When he did, I told him: 'The plan has changed slightly, sir. Sue Barker can't make it, but I've brought along a member of my staff. Do you mind if she stands in for Sue?' Edward had a very quick glance at Sophie, who was standing nearby, and said: 'Yes, that'll be fine', and that was it.

"There was no great interest at that stage, and they simply got on with the photo session. Sophie was wearing a sort of leotard under her sweater and there was a wonderful sequence where she quite naturally peeled off and then put on one sweatshirt after another as the pictures were taken. There was no royal protocol of any sort, either. Sophie leaned on Edward's shoulder as she posed with him, and there was no awe on her part and no great objection from him. They both behaved very naturally. I think its people like you and me who believe royalty shy away from that sort of behaviour, but Edward didn't bat an eyelid. He was smiling, laughing, loving every minute of it. Everything went very well, and when it was all over Sophie confided in me, in a very light-hearted way: 'I quite like him! We had a good laugh!' But I don't think for one moment she ever thought beyond that".

Below: A bewitched Edward appears captivated by Sophie. As she took over the management of the Real Tennis Challenge, the prince and the PR girl spent more and more time together.

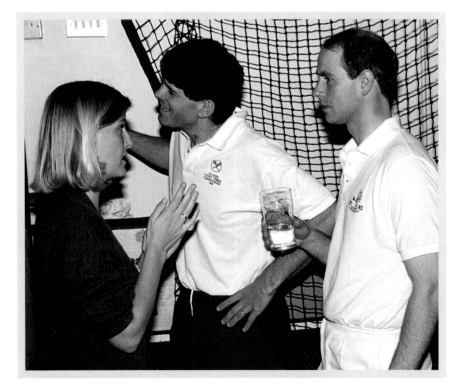

Love match

Prince Edward, though, obviously did, although there was not, as is often reported, an exchange of telephone numbers between Edward and Sophie after that first meeting. No calls. No messages. No nothing. But not long after the photo-session, Brian MacLaurin was invited to a breakfast meeting with the prince and his private secretary, Lieutenant-Colonel Sean O'Dwyer, at Edward's apartment in Buckingham Palace. "We had tea and croissants from a silver tray and discussed the next stage of the real tennis challenge", MacLaurin says, "and at the end of the meeting Prince Edward said to me, very casually and quietly: 'Do you think Sophie would have a game of tennis with me?' I said: 'I'm sure she'd love to, sir – why don't you ask her?'

> *"Sophie confided in me, 'I quite like him! We had a good laugh!'"*

"But after that I heard nothing. I'd say to Sophie in the office: 'Have you had an invitation to tennis yet?' and Prince Edward asked me again at another meeting: 'Do you think she'd have a game of tennis with me?', but still an invitation was not forthcoming. And at that stage I withdrew from day-to-day contact on the account and asked Sophie to take it on. That was not clandestine thinking on my part – just that I was very busy and it didn't need my constant management. But Sophie started giving it a lot of time and attention and began working quite closely with Edward to make the event a big success".

The Real Tennis Challenge, which raised some £30,000 for charity, was held in September 1993, and the following month Brian MacLaurin was invited to an end-of-the-event party with Edward and others involved. "I phoned the Palace and asked whether I could pass my invite to Sophie", he recalls, "and that was the night she got the first invitation to go out with Edward".

For their first date, the prince took Sophie to play real tennis and explain the arcane rules of the racket-and-ball indoor court game, first played in the monasteries and castle courtyards of France before the 12th century, and largely kept alive by the enthusiasm of French and English royals. Like

Henry VIII, who built a real tennis court at Hampton Court Palace around 1530 – and is said to have been playing there when told that Queen Anne Boleyn had been beheaded – Edward is a great aficionado. He wanted Sophie to share his passion for the sport, and one of his first gifts to her was a real tennis racket. "Edward decided to teach Sophie the game", says MacLaurin. "She went on to take lessons at Hampton Court, and is quite proficient at it now".

"But, like many things she did when she started seeing Edward, she kept it to her herself. There was never office gossip or discussion about their romance, and it wasn't even generally assumed that she was going out with Prince Edward. She did confide in me quite a lot, and I knew he took her to the theatre and cinema – things, strangely, I didn't think princes did, unless it was for some grand gala or première – and a lot of it had to be on the quiet, because there was no public awareness of their relationship. They went swimming, for example, in the Buckingham Palace pool, and met behind closed doors".

Sophie's beau

Anxious to keep their relationship secret, Edward and Sophie's courtship took place largely away from the public gaze. They had meetings in Sophie's West Kensington flat and also shared romantic meals in Edward's cramped second-floor Palace apartment. "It may be the best address in all England", an insider revealed, "but I wouldn't like to live there. It reminds me of a once-great hotel that is going to seed – all very grand and glamorous for guests, but with staff quarters that leave a lot to be desired".

Their rendezvous at the Palace made for greater intimacy, as Edward could dismiss his staff and they could spend time together alone. On their evenings out, however, Sophie had to become accustomed to having a "chaperone" with them, as Edward's private detective would be obliged to join them on dates.

The early stages of the couple's relationship, says Brian MacLaurin, "was a kind of slow burn. Sophie's personal life was her personal life, and she didn't communicate much about it to us. But she was entering a totally new and strange world, and clearly it would have been superhuman of her not to talk to someone about those early days. So she would occasionally confide to me little things, some

of her experiences – the first time Prince Philip kissed her, for example, and that kind of thing.

"She told me little stories, always greatly affectionate towards Edward and his family, and as the relationship grew she became an avid scholar of everything about them. She read all the books, scanned the newspapers, studied the histories of kings and queens, and became a huge fan of the Queen Mother and Prince Philip – she was always in awe of them – and latterly of Prince Charles, too. She was still in control and not at all bemused by

Above: Despite secretly dating a prince, Sophie's life appeared to carry on much as usual, and she revealed little of her new romance to friends or work colleagues.

Above: Brian MacLaurin escorts "Edward's girl" to her car, past hundreds of waiting photographers, as news of her relationship with the prince became public.

Opposite: Smiling Sophie during happier times at the Guards Polo Club. Despite the media attention, in some respects life was easier for Sophie once she could be seen out with Edward, rather than hiding in the shadows.

what was happening to her, and it was amazing how she became integrated with the royal family, and the closer she became to them, the more affection she displayed towards them.

"To me she was, and still is, the same girl, but I was perhaps more cautious about it all, because I feel like a big brother towards her, and I wanted her to stay in control and ensure that certain things didn't happen – that people who thought they might capitalize on her, for instance, did not do so". From those days, Brian MacLaurin has always kept a "brotherly" eye on his friend and former employee. "I've always played it down", he says. "I've been asked to do TV documentaries and a whole range of things, but I won't. Sophie has specifically asked her friends not to do those things. She says she doesn't want it. This book is quite different – I've spoken to her about it – because it's a celebration, and it would be madness for people not to help provide a factual record of their romance and marriage.

> *"In December came the day Sophie dreaded and can never forget"*

"Sophie is an intelligent girl who is totally in control of her own destiny and can make her own value judgements. But in those early days I sometimes wondered, with a degree of sympathy, how her parents felt, because I'm sure Christopher and Mary must have found the situation very difficult to accept. Considering the history of royal marriages as far as the public are concerned – I always say that, because we never know what really happened, only what newspapers say happened – it must have been difficult for them. I thought they may have been feeling 'Oh my God, what's our daughter got into?' But I always felt Sophie was moving towards a deeper relationship with a man she was clearly very fond of, and frankly it was none of my business. She could have been dating a prince or a pauper, and it really wasn't relevant as far as I was concerned".

The secret's out

For almost three months during 1993, through October, November and half of December, the royal romance stayed a secret. Edward, determined that Sophie would not to be given that "stigma" of being his girlfriend, used a code-name, often "Richard", when he phoned her office, and when he called to take her out, sent his detective to escort her to the car where he waited. It could not last, and in mid-December came the day Sophie dreaded and can never forget, when she knew the secret was out – and had been uncovered by Andrew Morton, who gained fame and considerable fortune with sensational revelations about the marriage of Prince Charles and the Princess of Wales in *Diana, Her True Story*.

"It was a Friday, just before Christmas", Brian MacLaurin recalls, "and a few of us were sitting around the office at about five in the evening when I suddenly looked up and thought 'Who's that guy?' Then I realized it was Andrew Morton, standing in the middle of the office! I still don't know how he got past our security – a barrier at the gates, locked doors and a manned reception area – but he just walked in, went straight up to Sophie at her desk and said 'Sophie Rhys-Jones, can I be the first person to call you Your Royal Highness?' It was like a bombshell. We were all stunned, and poor Sophie was in a state

Above: Packed for the weekend, Sophie escapes her London flat for the more illustrious surroundings of Windsor Castle. Her social life was now taking her into the upper echelons of the aristocracy.

Right: Pictured in the early stages of their romance, a casually dressed Edward and Sophie leave Buckingham Palace, flanked by the ubiquitous bodyguards.

of absolute shock. I whisked her away to the boardroom, and told her to stay there while I found out what was going on. I asked Morton: 'Andrew, what are you doing? You shouldn't be here', and he told me: 'I've got photographs of Sophie and Edward together, and of Edward leaving Sophie's place. I've been following them for weeks. I've got the whole story, and I just want to talk to Sophie'.

"So I left him with a couple of my staff, went back to tell Sophie the situation and we telephoned Prince Edward to discuss it with him. In the end, we agreed that Sophie should issue a short statement". It said simply: "Prince Edward and I are good friends and we work together. He is a private person and so am I. I have nothing more to add". That was more than enough for Morton – often called Clark Kent by his former colleagues for his resemblance to the Superman reporter – and he was escorted back through the security cordon which, with almost superhuman ingenuity, he'd managed to breach.

Now, with years of experience of his friends in the Press, MacLaurin knew he must get Sophie

away. He says: "I'd told Prince Edward on the phone 'I'll take her to my home' and we agreed to meet there, so we walked to my car in the underground car park and headed off. Sophie had calmed down and was fine, but as we drove away from the office I spotted three or four motorcyclists begin to follow and knew, of course, they were photographers out to get a picture". MacLaurin, equally determined that they would not, drove off in his Mazda sports car, leading the black-leathered lensmen on a crazy pursuit through the streets of west London.

"It wasn't at all fast or dangerous, and they followed at a discreet distance", he says, "but I found it quite exhilarating! As a former journalist, I found it extremely exciting and quite fun, and Sophie was sitting beside me laughing and quite relaxed, using the mobile phone to tell Edward – who was driving to meet us from central London – what was going on. They followed us for quite a way, but I managed to shake them off, except for one who stuck to me, hard on my tail, for a long time. So I pulled off the main road, drove straight onto Putney Heath and switched off the headlights – and we watched as he screamed straight past us!" At his home in Esher, Surrey, there was more laughter: "Soon after we arrived, Edward came to

collect Sophie", MacLaurin recalls. His wife, Gill, took having a prince of the realm in her living room "all in her stride". But as the couple were about to leave to spend the weekend at Windsor, MacLaurin's 18-year-old son, Peter, arrived home from work, opened the door and saw Prince Edward standing there looking at him. "He was absolutely speechless!", his father remembers, "and all he could say was a rather weak: 'Oh, hello'. Sophie saw his face and burst out laughing, and Edward joined in".

Making headline news

It was a joyous interlude in what would prove a traumatic weekend. Edward, furious that his privacy had been invaded, could only wait for the bombshell. It came on Sunday, when Morton's story

> "Sophie was very worried about what the impact of the news was going to be"

was splashed over *The News of the World*: "Edward in Love", it said, and predicted an early marriage at Westminster Abbey for the prince and "the girl of his dreams". The dream girl was equally devastated. That evening she returned to stay at the MacLaurin household to prepare herself for the following Monday morning – to face, for the first time, her new life in the public eye.

"Sophie was very worried that night about what the impact of the news was going to be", says MacLaurin, "and we got to the office early on Monday morning hoping to avoid the Press". Some hope. Fleet Street's finest had been on duty since dawn, and "as we approached the office there must have been a hundred journalists, TV cameramen and news photographers besieging the place. I knew they wouldn't go away until they got a picture of Sophie, but even though she was sitting by my side in the car, not one flashbulb went off!

"No-one really knew then what Sophie looked like, but there had been a story that she'd had her hair cut in a short style to try to look like Princess Diana. That was malicious rubbish, but not one photographer recognized her. I knew some of them very well, and one asked me: 'Where've you got her hidden, Brian – in the boot?' I tried to discreetly nod at her, to tip them the wink that *this* was the

Right: Edward and Sophie, all dressed up, attend a black tie function at the Park Lane Hilton in 1995. Increasingly, Sophie was accompanying the prince on more of his semi-official engagements.

Below: Sporty Sophie makes a splash at Cowes in 1994, when she learns to windsurf. At one point she is rescued from the sea by a boat full of watching photographers.

WEEKENDS AT WINDSOR

Meeting The Firm and how Sophie fitted in

For any girlfriend, meeting a potential mother-in-law can be an intimidating experience. When that mother is the Queen, it must be a terrifying prospect. Even that, though, is a situation catered for by royal tradition: "Queen Victoria", Elizabeth Longford writes in her book *Royal Throne: The Future of the Monarchy*, "used to invite each of her future daughters-in-law to pay her 'a little visit' at Windsor before marriage. The ostensible reason was that she could get to know them. I suspect that the real reason was for them to get to know her, the Queen, and the ways and traditions of the royal family".

It was the same for Sophie, who met Edward's mother on one of her first weekend visits to Windsor. The prearranged meeting took place over a nerve-wracking lunch with the Queen, Prince Philip, Princess Anne and her husband Tim Laurence. After weeks

of agonizing over this important moment and practising her royal curtsy, it was all over in a flash. Within a very short space of time Sophie was totally accepted – and, more importantly, liked and appreciated – by the royal family. The Queen's now-famous first appraisal of her, "You wouldn't notice her in a crowd", might seem to some to be a devastating putdown, but, after the massive media attention surrounding (and, some say, sought by) Princess Diana and Sarah Ferguson, it was high praise for Sophie. "That's the way she likes it", says a friend.

Above: Sophie's warmth and caring nature soon made her a favourite with the Queen Mother.

Left: The Queen and Sophie at a canter in Windsor Park. Sophie improved her equestrian skills after learning that horseriding jaunts were a regular part of royal relaxation.

She may be a positive person, but she's ot at all pushy".

She is also, as her former teachers nd employers all agreed, a girl who earns fast – and as well as taking up and mastering some of Edward's favourite astimes, like windsurfing and real ennis, she learned the strict rules of tiquette at the royal homes. "No one, or instance, is allowed to go to bed efore the Queen or Princess Margaret", ngrid Seward reveals in her biography f Edward. "There is an order for ntering the dining room at mealtimes, nd while the Queen Mother, the Queen nd Princess Margaret can drink as much as they like (and on occasion do ust that), anyone who is so foolish s to try and keep pace with them will find their bags packed and waiting in the hall the following morning".

Sophie learned those rules very early on, and after a while was regularly invited to go out horse-riding with the Queen. She was also accorded the rare privilege of driving with her to church – an honour which is only bestowed on someone who is "engaged" to a family member – and a "special access" pass to all royal residences.

But, despite widespread belief, she was not given her own apartment at Buckingham Palace until after the engagement announcement, when she went out of her way to tell the media that "Contrary to popular opinion, we have never lived together".

Sophie and Edward tried to escape from the limelight whenever they could, relaxing together at Windsor. This is where he feels most at home, with a more spacious apartment – two bedrooms, two bathrooms and a sitting-room – on the top floor of the Queen's Tower, complete with its own private entrance. Even out of the public eye, however, they were not safe from prying lenses, and when a photographer snapped them kissing during a Scottish holiday, Edward protested to the Press Complaints Commission and received apologies from most of the newspapers which published the picture.

Despite such unwelcome intrusion, the romance flourished. Gradually and quietly, Sophie Rhys-Jones became an apprentice member of The Firm. She

regularly joined Edward and his family for holidays at Sandringham and Balmoral, and as a guest on the royal yacht *Britannia*. She also increasingly accompanied the prince on semi-official engagements and helped with his charitable work on the Duke of Edinburgh Award scheme, for which he raises some £3 million a year.

"If she had wished", writes Ingrid Seward, "the Queen could have terminated the affair, or at least made it very difficult to continue by making it clear to Prince Edward that she would not welcome Sophie in any of her royal houses. That she did not is a measure of her approval, and Sophie became ever more assimilated into Edward's way of life".

Above: Edward and Sophie accompany Prince Philip and Princess Margaret to church at Sandringham, after New Year's festivities.

Centre: Windsor Castle, Edward's favourite royal residence and weekend retreat.

Left: An informal moment, as Edward and Sophie arrive for a summer break at Balmoral.

girl, hoping they'd get a quick shot and go away. But not one took the hint, and we drove on without a single picture being taken".

The photographers' fury at themselves for missing a "sitting duck" was equalled only by the wrath of their newspaper bosses. "I know at least two of them got a tremendous dressing down from their editor", smiles MacLaurin, "but it didn't solve our problem. We were still besieged, and I knew they wouldn't go away.

"I phoned Prince Edward and pleaded with him to let us do something positive. He was all for doing nothing, but I argued that Sophie and I had to continue to work with these journalists, and after a long discussion he agreed that I should make a statement. So I went outside – it was pouring with rain and freezing cold – and told the Press that the friendship of Edward and Sophie was a new one. I said: 'It might work, it might not work, but please give them the space and privacy to work it out'."

Edward issued a similar statement, adding "I am very conscious that other members of m family have been subjected to similar attention, an it has not been at all beneficial to thei relationships". Within hours, London's *Evenin Standard* ran a story headlined "Edward: Give u a Break!" Still, though, there were no pictures of th girl in question. "The reporters had their story, bu the photographers were still massed outside", Bria MacLaurin remembers, "and I persuaded Princ Edward to let me walk Sophie to a car so they coul get their shots and leave her alone.

"By now police had set up barriers around th office, with the photographers behind them, an before we went out, I told Sophie: 'When we get t the car, look down the line of photographers, coun five slowly in your head, and then get in. That wi give them all the chance to get pictures and positio yourself professionally with those guys forever They'll appreciate what you're doing for them And that's exactly what she did. Although sh

Below: Edward and Sophie appear happy and relaxed at the annual Windsor Horse Show. As their courtship continued, Sophie was no longer perceived as just "Edward's girl", but half of a royal couple.

was very nervous, she looked cool and calm and did it to perfection.

"We then disappeared off to our office Christmas party – a bit of a laugh. But that was how the news first broke, and of course Sophie has never been out of the spotlight since". It was far from a situation she relished: "Sophie was upset at the beginning by all the media attention", her father revealed in a rare interview, with his local newspaper, "because she just wants a quiet life". There was now little chance of that.

Above: Chauffeur-driven, Sophie and Edward take a back seat as Prince Philip drives the family to church.

Princess in waiting?

Despite the couple's misgivings about their relationship becoming public knowledge, their romance continued to blossom, and Sophie's foray into the realm of royalty opened up a new and fascinating world of privilege and protocol. Only a few weeks after the news story broke, Sophie found herself as a house guest at Sandringham for the Queen's traditional New Year's Eve party. This is a relatively relaxed affair, with a gathering of family and old friends, and activities usually revolving around riding, shooting, and a film screening in the ballroom. Sophie's invitation to the house party was a strong indication that she had found favour with the Queen, and she would now move as a regular in royal circles.

With his mother's seal of approval for his steady girlfriend, Edward wanted to make his intentions clear and show his commitment to Sophie. However, the prince was reluctant to rush into announcing a wedding, especially after the recent string of broken marriages from his older siblings. Also, he didn't want to be pressured into a proposal by eager Press speculation. But he and Sophie, it is believed, agreed to be very unofficially "engaged", until they were both ready to marry.

In the meantime, the working couple continued to focus on their business ambitions, establishing their careers on a stronger footing.

Right: Dressed in a fur-trimmed suit and hat, Sophie accompanies the rest of the royals at the Queen and Prince Philip's 50th wedding anniversary celebrations, held at the Royal Naval College in Greenwich, London.

Chapter Six

PATHS TO SUCCESS

A creative and talented couple, Edward and Sophie excel in their chosen careers

P rince Edward, unlike Sophie, made a few false starts in life before finding his true vocation. Resolved to make his own independent way in life, he won his parents' approval to start a career in the theatre, and began his working life as "the royal teaboy" with Andrew Lloyd Webber's Really Useful Theatre Group, rising to coordinate its overseas productions. Then, after a brief interlude with a new, independent theatre company, he found his true niche in television.

The prince set up his own production company, named Ardent, worked hard to learn the tricks of the television trade, and eventually became known as a "tough cookie" in business matters, as well as a skilled and natural presenter of his own TV programmes.

Sophie, meanwhile, was juggling the demands of her career as a PR executive with those of being "Edward's girlfriend", constantly having to deal with stories about herself, rather than her own clients. In the end she, too, set up her own company because, she said: "I decided it was important, as far as my working life was concerned, to be in charge of my own destiny".

Once they were both established and successful in their chosen professions, it was then time to turn to more personal affairs, as Edward made plans to whisk Sophie away for a pre-Christmas holiday on a romantic Caribbean island.

Left: Edward has found his true niche working as an executive producer making television programmes. Here he oversees the film crew shooting a scene for *Real Tennis*, Ardent's first documentary.

"The theatre would be a perfect vehicle for his talents"

I n a *Crown and Country* TV documentary (written and presented by Edward Windsor; executive producer Edward Windsor), the Queen's youngest son strolls around the imposing Norman and Tudor Carisbrooke Castle above Newport on the Isle of Wight, and tells how one governor of the island started life as a whipping boy for the future King Henry VIII. "It was a crime to offer violence to a prince of the blood", Edward explains, "and to get round this a boy was appointed to take the punishment if the prince did anything wrong". Then he shrugs his shoulders, looks straight to camera and adds with mock gravity: "Regrettably, the practice has long been abolished".

Joker in the pack

It's a neat, nice touch of self-mockery, prompting the appalling thought that any wretched lad hired to suffer for Edward's conceived misdemeanours would have been lashed to within an inch of his life. For after the adverse publicity over his departure from the Marines came another setback to the prince's public profile with *It's a Royal Knockout*, masterminded by Edward and blamed for severely damaging the image of the royal family. Originally planned to raise money for the Duke of Edinburgh Award scheme, it was officially named "The Grand Charity Knockout Tournament" and based on a popular TV programme of outdoor fun, frolics, games and challenges, which Edward loved as a child. He put everything into its planning, recruiting sister Anne, and brother Andrew and his wife Sarah, to dress in medieval costumes and join him as team leaders of a host of celebrities who competed against each other in aid of four charities.

Filmed at Alton Towers fun park in June 198? (and watched by 18 million TV viewers the follow-ing week), it was a nightmare, from summer rai turning the site to a muddy morass to the Press' final damning verdict of what *The Times* calle "the royal family's love of pantomime taken to nev heights of carefully-controlled silliness". An Edward added to the problem when he met th media, who had been cooped up all day. "Thank for being so bloody enthusiastic!", the prince raile at them before, as one report said, "flouncing ou like a ballerina with a hole in his tights" .

With *Knockout* behind him, it was now tim for Edward to put away the joker-in-the-pack su and think seriously about his future. The theatre he had decided, would be a perfect vehicle for hi talents, although achieving, or being allowed t achieve, that ambition seemed a distant dream.

A "Really Useful" job

For the Queen's 60th birthday in 1986, Edwar staged a celebration production at Windsor of humorous mini-operetta called (and all about *Cricket*, written for him by composer Andrew Lloyd Webber and lyricist Tim Rice, who penne

Right: Edward's charitable cause, *It's a Royal Knockout*, raised money and provided entertainment, but at the expense of royal dignity, according to some commentators.

Opposite, bottom right: Edward jests about his own identity, but has found that a prince's efforts are often judged more harshly.

such immensely-successful musicals as *Evita* and *Jesus Christ Superstar*. Planning the event brought him in to contact with Biddy Hayward, executive director of Lloyd Webber's Really Useful Theatre Group, and they became firm friends. Later, when Edward confided to her his unhappiness with the Marines and his desire to work in theatre, Hayward went into action and,

> ## *"He will have to make the tea and answer the telephones"*

after a series of meetings – not least with the prince's parents – Buckingham Palace announced in January 1988 that Prince Edward would join the group as a production assistant.

But what exactly would he be *doing* in the job, which paid no more than £10,000 a year? "Like the rest of us he will have to make the tea and answer the telephones", Hayward told reporters. "He will have no special status, and is starting on the lowest

rung of the ladder". Inevitably, Edward was dubbed the "Really Useful royal teaboy" and the following month, displaying that often-hidden hint of humour and aptitude for self-mockery, duly turned up for his first day of work at the appropriately-named Palace Theatre in London's West End clutching, for the benefit of assembled photographers, a box of PG Tips teabags.

He *did* make the tea, too – as well as eventually helping coordinate overseas productions of Lloyd Webber's shows, from advertising to box-office sales to marketing merchandise. He made new friends in the company, often sharing a typical office worker's lunch in the bistros and cheap and cheerful cafes of Soho. He adopted for the first time the "ordinary" name of Edward Windsor, fitted in well, and thoroughly enjoyed working in live theatre. But it was a short-lived experience.

In June 1990, Biddy Hayward parted company with Lloyd Webber after an internal dispute and soon afterwards six other members of the staff, including Edward, resigned and joined her in a new venture. There was talk of mutiny, conspiracy and a clandestine midnight meeting to plot the "mass desertion", but Lloyd

Above left: The prince's first working day as plain "Edward Windsor".

Above right: Edward with Glenn Close and Andrew Lloyd Webber at a showing of *Sunset Boulevard*. The prince still has a keen love of the theatre.

Above: Sophie lands a job as a PR executive, a position that would take her around the country organizing launches, and also into the arms of a prince.

Right: The man behind Edward's decision to work in television, Malcolm Cockren has been a stalwart supporter and a great admirer of the prince's achievements.

Webber said very little, except through a spokesman: "These things happen in any business and it is a good move for the people concerned. He wishes them well". Edward declared himself "particularly grateful" to Lloyd Webber's theatre group "for their support and encouragement over the past couple of years and especially for giving me the chance to work in the theatre professionally. I hope to use the experience to progress further into production and explore new areas". However, those areas, explored with the new Theatre Division company, were to provide only another setback for Edward's budding theatrical ambitions.

With London audiences dwindling because of economic recession, and further diminished by the Gulf War, the struggling new company planned a fightback with a costly revival of *Billy*, based on Keith Waterhouse's classic 1959 novel *Billy Liar*. "They talked for some time about reviving *Billy* as a musical", Waterhouse reveals. "But like many of those projects it just seemed to peter out". So, too, did Theatre Division: it folded in July 1991, leaving debts of some £600,000 and Edward Windsor once again seeking gainful employment.

He turned for advice to, among others, Malcolm Cockren, a Hertfordshire-born businessman with a level-headed approach to the entertainment world and a wealth of hard-won experience of both making and insuring films. Cockren, whose insurance-brokering company has covered every major player in Hollywood for more than thirty years, recalled: "Prince Edward and I met during that infamous but hugely successful *Royal Knockout* tournament, when I arranged the insurance and looked after all the transport and operational movements".

Both men still have mixed feelings about that particular event: "In certain ways it understandably caught the wrath of the public and Press", Cockren admits. "Everyone looked at it as a rather stupid game session and ignored the good it did for many, many people. What has never been really explained – probably because of an oversight by the PR people – is that in a few hours we raised more than £1,500,000 for four charities. For them, it was a huge success, and to raise that amount in such a short time says much for Edward's organizational abilities".

Career advice, by appointment

Malcolm Cockren was to see much more of those abilities when the prince invited him to join his Special Projects Group (SPG), part of the Duke of Edinburgh Award scheme. "It was a very small team, just six or eight people and mainly close pals from his Cambridge days", he says, "but Edward and I hit it off during the *Knockout* tournament and I think he needed to expand his team. We tried to devise innovative ways of persuading people that they *wanted* to give us money, and there's no doubt that Edward can come up with some stupendous ideas. Once, for instance, he said almost flippantly: 'Why don't you borrow the QE2?' and in a very short space of time I'd got Cunard's agreement to hold a magnificent party on the liner in Southampton. It raised £150,000 in one evening, and was so successful that we did it again a couple of years later and raised a similar sum".

The prince's group, which collected some £3 million over five years, was disbanded – though it could reassemble at any time to mount special charity events – when its members found their careers taking up more of their time. Career matters were top of Edward Windsor's agenda, too. "When it was decided he was no longer going to partake of the Civil List", says Cockren, "Edward realized that to have a life he could be proud of he would have to work for a living. I think both the Queen and the Duke of Edinburgh probably envisaged he'd have a future in perhaps the legal profession or accountancy. When he said: 'Well, I'm going to have to go to work', I think it was expected he would move into an acknowledged profession, but of course he wasn't interested in those, and that's where I came in.

"He'd had a taste of theatre life and liked it and had made a very conscious decision to work in the entertainment industry. My experience was very useful in Edward's thinking and he just wanted advice on what he should do and thoughts on how he might progress his life. He and I gave it a great deal of thought over many, many months and meetings, and because of my cinema background he said: 'I suppose you would recommend that I go into films'. But I told him: 'No, I don't think you should. Film is far too risky. You can have a great time in the film industry, as I have done, but running your own shop is very different from running a Hollywood company'. I also cautioned him that theatre was not the way, because you can have a single great success but a hundred failures.

"I advised: 'Concentrate on television, which gives far greater flexibility – still with massive potential, but of a size which allows you to run your own business'. He accepted that totally and we set about deciding when, what and how. Again we met over a long period, sometimes every day, and quite obviously he had to discuss these things with his parents and I think at one time the prime minister, to keep him informed, as a matter of courtesy, of what he was doing".

"He made a conscious decision to work in the entertainment industry"

Above: Despite their busy work schedules, Edward finds time to turn up and support the ambitious Sophie at some of her more important launches.

Above: Business executive Edward Windsor pauses for a time-check on his way to the office, on the day that Ardent Productions is officially launched.

An Ardent businessman

With, once again, his parents' full approval, Edward set about forming his company, with Malcolm Cockren as chairman, himself joint managing director along with Eben Foggitt, a barrister and TV executive, and Malcolm Eldridge as finance director. The prince learned essential skills of how to compile a business plan, choose the firm's initial employees and, most importantly, find financial backers. With £205,000 of his own invested, he sought some £750,000 more and, it is widely believed, found the immensely-wealthy Sultan of Brunei a willing supporter. But "shareholders are people we never discuss", says Cockren. "They are people I respect enormously and who have shown a great deal of trust in us – delightful and first-class individuals who are friends as well as business colleagues. Part of our agreement is that we never talk about them, and we never will".

He will talk, however, about the early days of Ardent – a name Edward came up with after Cockren advised him that "people looking in a directory sometimes never get further than A, B or C". Then the prince set about learning his new trade and, like everything he does, threw himself into the task with vigour. "We had to start from absolute rock bottom", Cockren recalls, "developing ideas and associations and contacts. Above all, Edward had to go over two years of a severe learning curve to assimilate all the information he possibly could from a host of established people who were kind enough to offer their assistance".

Approval ratings

With a small staff and smart London headquarters at Ariel House, Charlotte Street, in the heart of TV-land off Tottenham Court Road, fledgling Ardent Productions took its first tentative steps into the tough world of independents for the first time in 1993. However, the company received an early setback that critics still drag up today: "We were beginning to get quite well known for factual programmes", says Malcolm Cockren (one was, inevitably, on real tennis), "but we wanted to see profits coming sooner and had the opportunity to talk to Channel Four about a drama idea which might help us achieve that".

The idea was for *Annie's Bar*, a topical satirical sitcom set in the House of Commons, written with the help of political journalists and members of parliament, some of whom agreed to appear as themselves. "Channel Four commissioned half a dozen scripts and gave us a deadline of perhaps nine months", Cockren adds, "but very soon afterwards they said they had a slot for it in three months' time – or maybe never at all. And in our anxiety to please them and get our first major drama programme off the ground, we went for that three-month option. It was, on reflection, an impossibility, and everything suffered". With fewer than a million viewers, *Annie's Bar* was judged a flop and axed after the first series.

But a big breakthrough came with *Edward on Edward*, produced to commemorate the 60th anniversary of the abdication of Edward VIII. It was, said the prince, "the story of Edward, Duke of Windsor's exile from his homeland, and my own personal search to find out more about the great uncle I never knew". And Edward gave it everything, says leading photographer Paul Massey, who

watched him at work on the project. "I spent nine months going all over the world with him", Massey recalls, "and though we began with a full TV crew, eventually it got down to just Edward, me and his detective. So he had to muck in, and he didn't mind at all. Once, at Madrid airport, when I was rushing around sorting out tickets, he picked up my camera bags and ran to the plane with them!

"Another time, for a special picture, I left a message at Windsor asking if he could wear something different from the outfit he'd worn all the time for continuity in the film. He rang me back – "Hello, it's Edward" – and asked *me* what he should wear. He knew there was a job to do, understood the problem and wanted to know the best way to do it". Massey enjoyed Edward's company: "He's a very pleasant guy, not at all as some people perceive

"He picked up my camera bags and ran to the plane with them!"

him. He's not aloof, and certainly not gay or wimpish, but very much a private person. And I was surprised how very good he is at dealing with people, from Arab leaders we met in Dubai to ordinary folk. He was absolutely brilliant, very impressive, with them. Oddly enough, though, he hates having his photograph taken, and I got the strong feeling that he'd love not to be the focus of all that attention. It makes him feel uncomfortable, and I think he'd really like to just slip off and be in the background, and be himself."

Edward on Edward received mixed reviews in Britain, but was a huge international success. "It was a major turning point", says Ardent chairman Malcolm Cockren, "because it was the first programme known around the world as an

Above: Another royal documentary, *Crown and Country*, is fronted by the prince. To his credit, he has been lauded as a natural in front of the camera and a talented presenter.

Below: Although Edward is usually credited as executive producer, he has learned about all aspects of film-making, from camera work to negotiating rights.

Ardent quality programme. We'd made numerou others, but this had a high impact, because it was a subject which fascinates people everywhere". On the strength of that documentary, the American TV network CBS paid Ardent £2.5 million for a serie on American dynasties, including the Gettys and the Kennedys.

At home, though, it generated claims that Edward had "cashed in" by using his roya connections – something he'd said at the outset he would never do. Cockren responds: "We have neve wanted to concentrate on royal programmes, or be known as a royal programme-maker, and ou output then, now and planned for the future clearly shows that. But because of Edward's connection it's inevitable that we are asked to make programmes featuring royalty in some way. It would be absurd for Ardent not to do so, because we are in a quite unique position to achieve a bette programme than probably anyone else in the world Why wouldn't people want us to take advantage o such a situation? We haven't done our best to keep away from royal programmes, or to go for them We've just let it happen when it makes sense, and if we do that honestly, I can't see the problem".

For Edward, it was another example of the difficulties he faces in trying to do his own thing "Sometimes, as I've said, he can do no right", say Cockren, "and it must be very dispiriting, especially when he knows, and I know, and those close to him know, that he couldn't possibly have achieved more. Just occasionally you see his exasperation a some situation like that, but it's a very human and understandable reaction when you realize how disheartening it must be for him".

The future of television

After the *Edward on Edward* accolades, Arden seemed set for a fair future, with aims to be among Britain's top 12 independent production companie by the end of the century. As 1999 began, the prince declared: "We are about to enter the busies year of our existence. It has been building over the last year, and suddenly we are looking at an enormous workload".

Richard Simons, Director of Programmes a Meridian television, is deeply impressed with the presenter prince and how far he has come since his early Ardent days. Simons recalls: "We first met when I was commissioning editor at Carlton TV and 'Edward Windsor' came in to pitch some ideas

A PROPOSAL IN PARADISE

At last, Edward offers his hand in marriage

Above: On the idyllic Bahamian island of Windermere, thousands of miles away from the royal family and the Press, Edward finally takes the plunge and asks Sophie if she will do him the honour of being his wife.

Back home, Britain was bracing itself for Christmas and the cold, ice and snow of winter … and on an idyllic, all-but-deserted sub-tropical island, where the Atlantic rolls on to pink-hued coral beaches, Edward at last asked the question that Sophie (and millions more) had been waiting for: "Will you marry me?"

The prince had laid his plans well. He arranged to take Sophie on a brief pre-Christmas Caribbean break to the holiday home of family friends the Duke and Duchess of Abercorn, on Windermere Island in the Bahamas. It's an area well known to royals: a slightly-smiling Queen Victoria still sits enthroned in stone in Nassau, the to us. He was absolutely charming, with a very helpful humility, in that he was new to the game and wanted to learn everything from you.

"When I met him again not many years later, he was much sharper and tougher, and knew what he was doing in terms of business. He's a real tough cookie to deal with. In programmes, I think he needs a strong creative and editorial presence to work with, because that's not his real forte, but as a presenter he has come of age. He is totally at ease with the camera, and has the ability of all the best presenters of being able to convey a real and credible enthusiasm for his subject. And when it comes to programmes like *Crown and Country* he's far better than most, because he knows his subject. So he has a sort of double whammy – he's quite natural in front of camera, knows what he's talking about and commands attention. He has a very real talent".

"He is totally at ease with the camera and conveys a real enthusiasm"

Ardent staff insist that, despite what some say, Edward researches and writes the programmes he presents: "We're too small a company for him to be anything but hard-working and very good at his job". Despite dedication and long hours, Edward was still sniped at for his company's supposed lack

Above: Showing her caring side, Sophie chats to a youngster at an open day for Airborne, a charity which gives disabled children the chance to fly.

of success, with estimated losses of £1.5 million, while reportedly giving himself a 20 per cent pay rise. Malcolm Cockren responds: "Why don't these people get their facts right? We have had a loss every year, but they were expected and budgeted, and came as no surprise to anyone in the company or our shareholders. They were exactly as predicted in our business plan; we didn't expect to make money in the early years.

"But our projections are almost on target, and I think that at long last our figures finally indicate a profit, which will vindicate our decisions and commitment to quality. Similarly, a lot of rubbish is written about Edward and his salary. Some newspapers have put it in the order of £120,000 a year. That's nonsense! However, whatever his salary, he more than earns it, because he is doing a thunderingly good job in an industry renowned for being difficult".

Sophie Rhys-Jones, meanwhile, was facing problems in her own career, not least in June 1994 when journalist James Whitaker wrote in the *Mirror* that her romance with Edward was off.

Left: Ace of hearts? Sophie's work often finds her in glamorous surroundings, fitting for a future royal. Here she is pictured at the Regain Trust Spring Charity Ball.

Bahamian capital and main port; and the Duke of Windsor was the islands' governor during World War II – a post without precedence for a member of Britain's royal family.

Later, the family's much-missed "Uncle Dickie" Mountbatten, and then Prince Charles and Diana, discovered the allure of Windermere, an exclusive paradise just five miles long, and reached only by a short bridge from the much larger island of Eleuthera. Apart from its breathtaking beauty, Windermere's main attraction for well-heeled visitors – who have included Jackie Onassis and Henry Kissinger, among many other international celebrities – is the complete privacy it offers (and the security guards, who keep watch on the bridge to deter unwelcome tourists).

"Of course the main draw is the setting", says Ricardo Bovero, manager of the ultra-smart Windermere Club, built by home-owners as a dining and sporting venue. "This is one of the most beautiful and, yes, most romantic, spots on earth. A magical place, with pink sands and turquoise water, wonderful for snorkelling, windsurfing and fishing". Ricardo believes the island is paradise on earth: "It's also a very private place. There are fewer than 50 homes here, and people come to get away from it all and feel they're on a deserted island. You are left alone, no-one bothers you, and that's its other big attraction".

It was plainly the place for Edward when he at last proposed. Why, he was asked a few weeks later, had he delayed? "It's impossible for anyone else to understand why it has taken me this long", he said, "but I don't think it would have been right before, and I don't think Sophie would have said yes before". And the fact that she did say yes, he added, meant "I must have got the timing right".

With the timing, and the setting, perfect, Edward was finally ready to pop the all-important question to Sophie. "I managed to take her completely by surprise", he said. "She had no idea that it was coming, which is what I really wanted to do". Sophie's reaction: "I was slightly stunned for a minute. Then I suddenly realized I should actually answer the question. I said: 'Yes. Yes please!'"

For a proposal of marriage, there couldn't be a more romantic place, says Jackie Kemp, who has looked after visitors on the island for 21 years: "In the afternoons, when the sun is setting, the fine white sand turns a beautiful pink hue, and in the evenings the sky is very clear and the stars are bright and it's very, very beautiful".

Even here, in this little Eden, they had followed the progress of the royal romance and, although the island's strict code of privacy forbids any discussion of guests, Jackie smiles: "If the couple were here, I'm sure they'll come back. We all certainly hope so".

Below: A sign in Nassau indicates the myriad of small islands which make up the Bahamas.

Bottom: The islands are renowned for their breathtaking scenery, and they are also a mecca for watersports enthusiasts, like Edward and Sophie.

Above: All smiles at Ardent as business is flourishing. Prince Edward has now abandoned his London base and works from the converted stables in his new home at Bagshot Park.

Left: Bearing a bouquet of flowers, Sophie leaves her job at MacLaurin Communications in December 1995, to set up her own PR venture.

"She was very upset", her former PR boss Brian MacLaurin remembers, "and I sat her down and said: 'Sorry to ask you this – but is it true?' She said 'Well, no – I was with Edward last night'.

"We were at an airfield in Buckinghamshire for a Press call, and had expected only a handful of journalists to turn up, but of course the 'story' brought them flocking there. So Sophie and I prepared a little speech, and when they asked if her romance was off, she said: 'I am always amazed at what I read in the papers, which is why I love my job and the media so much. One day they can be right, and the next so wrong – who knows?' I told her to say it with a smile, say nothing more and leave it in the air. She did exactly that, and completely defused the whole situation".

Career conflicts

Even so, Sophie's dual role, as career woman and prince's girlfriend, continued to create problems. "Instead of being just a PR executive, she was now herself a story", says MacLaurin, "and people were constantly phoning and hassling her with personal questions which had absolutely nothing to do with her job. Over a couple of years there were many occasions when we had to sit down and discuss how to handle the latest 'story' about her.

"About 99 per cent of them were absolute rubbish and obviously made up, and I read them with amazement. But this was going on day after day, and Sophie had to take time off from her job to deal with them. She managed all these things very well, but they were very time-consuming and she'd get very upset and take a bit of calming down. In reality, it began to work against Sophie and her career".

Nor was Sophie the only one to suffer: "When so-called 'stories' broke in the papers, I became concerned that maybe someone within the company was leaking stuff to them, because in our business we talk to journalists all the time. That suspicion, however groundless, must have been there with Sophie and Edward, too, so we became slightly compromised". To solve the problem, her boss first changed Sophie's working routine, giving her an extra day off each week so she could become acclimatized to her new role and lifestyle, and then talking over what she could do in the future.

"We eventually agreed that it would be sensible for her to start up something herself", says MacLaurin, "in which she would not have to be in day-to-day contact with journalists, but could use her position of interest to be a focus of business and have other people around her to deal with the Press. We had a kind of agreement in which she and I knew she probably couldn't continue with us, and we worked for about 18 months towards this idea of her setting up on her own. We talked about it and looked at various options and decided that was the answer".

Sophie branches out

Sophie set up her own company, R-JH Public Relations, with partner Murray Harkin, after she'd left MacLaurin and freelanced for a few months. She launched it, she said, "because if I joined another company a lot of employees would think I'd got the job only because of my personal situation. I decided it was important, as far as my working life was concerned, to be in charge of my own destiny".

Even so, she was sad to leave MacLaurin Communications. On her last day, in December 1995, her boss again escorted her, with a farewell bouquet, to a waiting car, as he'd done when she first hit the headlines. Sophie, professional as ever, told assembled photographers she didn't know what all the fuss was about. "I'm just changing jobs", she smiled.

Brian MacLaurin points to a picture on his office wall of that farewell day: "It was a completely amicable and delightful parting of the ways", he says. "We had a little office party and said our goodbyes, but we stay good friends and very much in touch, lunching regularly and talking on the phone a lot. Sophie has a great little business, specializing in luxury goods and products, as well as high-profile launches which are attracted to the advantages Sophie can bring.

"And she certainly knows the media and how to deal with them – with respect and an understanding that they have a job to do, but with caution, because she knows some can get up to odd little tricks to get a good picture. She can second-guess what they're going to do, which can't do her any harm in her new royal role".

Right: Highly amused, Sophie enjoys herself at the Baby Lifeline charity fashion show. With her new company, she no longer has direct contact with the Press, though she has won some prestigious clients, including jewellers Boodle and Dunthorpe and the Lanesborough Hotel.

Chapter Seven

RULES OF ENGAGEMENT

With only six months to go, the race was on to organize the wedding of the year

At last Edward was ready to marry and Sophie had accepted his proposal with an enthusiastic "Yes please!". And then, after seeking the approval of their parents, they announced their joyful news to the world from the blossom-filled gardens of St James's Palace.

As Sophie – and her family – were thrust into the limelight, she learned for the first time what it really meant to be a engaged to a prince. Wherever she went – to the ski-slopes, receptions or other friends' weddings – she was photographed and had her wardrobe scrutinized by so-called "experts". She posed with Edward for a wedding-day stamp, watched with amusement as Sophie Rhys-Jones "lookalikes" appeared on the books of model agencies and, after the murder of her TV-presenter friend Jill Dando, reluctantly accepted that she, like Edward, would have to live shadowed by an armed bodyguard.

As for any bride, it was a hectic time, overseeing the final touches to her new home at Bagshot Park, making guest and wedding-present lists and choosing flowers, having final fittings for her gown, trying on the wedding ring. She found there were a thousand-and-one little things to do before the big day, and the time between January and June just seemed to fly by …

Left: A month before the wedding, Sophie appears in a contemplative mood, as the bride-to-be and her prince relax at the Windsor Horse Show.

"The Queen and Prince Philip were thrilled and delighted"

It was the news the world had waited five years to hear – but when it came, it was still a big surprise to even many friends and courtiers. With the Queen still on holiday at Sandringham, and the royal Press pack covering the Prince of Wales on a Swiss skiing holiday, no big news was expected from Buckingham Palace. But at 10 am on Wednesday January 6, 1999, came an official statement: "The Queen and the Duke of Edinburgh are delighted to announce the engagement of their youngest son, Prince Edward, to Miss Sophie Rhys-Jones". Both families, it added, "are thrilled at the news".

For Edward, it had taken weeks of careful planning. First, he had spirited Sophie away to Windermere Island for the proposal. Sophie was stunned – her hairstylist, Andrew Collinge, said she had no idea of the marriage plan when she had visited his Knightsbridge salon just days before her Bahamas break. Then the couple flew back to wintry Britain and, between Christmas and the New Year, told their parents the good news. First Edward informed the Queen – and she and Prince Philip were "thrilled and delighted" to finally hear the news they'd been expecting for at least three years. In fact, it's said his mother had even warned Edward that if he didn't propose soon, he would lose Sophie.

Not long afterwards, the prince, displaying old-fashioned style and chivalry, drove to Brenchley to formally ask Sophie's father if he might marry his daughter. "He asked my permission, and I was delighted. He's a very nice chap", beamed Christopher Rhys-Jones as he and wife Mary were thrust into the media spotlight. They enjoyed Edward's company, they said, and were very, very happy for the "wonderful couple". Finally came the official announcement, and soon afterwards the couple strolled hand in hand towards the cameras in the gardens of St James's Palace, to talk publicly for the first time about their love, their marriage and their future.

A royal announcement

The unusually mild January day had brought out the blossom on the trees, and the watery sun highlighted the glittering detail on Sophie's slate-grey Tomasz Starzewski suit and the ring on her finger – three stunning diamonds set in 18-carat white gold. Commissioned by Edward from royal jeweller Asprey & Garrard of Bond Street, and estimated to have cost around £105,000, the "simple yet modern" ring features a 2.05-carat oval diamond flanked by two smaller heart-shaped gems, set in white gold. It is believed to be the most expensive engagement ring in royal history.

Asked about the ring, Edward joked: "Well, it's that funny thing on Sophie's ring finger, actually. Quite sparkly. Diamonds are a girl's best friend, so I'm told". Sophie laughingly protested: "No! You're my best friend!" It was, observant commentators noted, a break from the traditional yellow gold and

Right: Prince Edward presents his fiancée, as is custom, at a photo-call in the gardens of St James's Palace. The announcement brightened up a wintry day, as the British nation looked forward to a summer royal wedding.

weighty style of other royal engagement rings, and very different from
the sapphire and diamond sported
by the Princess of Wales on a similar
day in 1981.

But then this Sophie was a very
different girl. Where Diana had
giggled and bashfully lowered her
head, Sophie was confident and
outgoing, handling the Press, as she
has learned to, with respect laced
with caution. And from Edward there
was none of Prince Charles's hesitant
awkwardness when he had faced
the media and, asked if he was in
love, uttered four words that would
return to haunt him again and again:
"Whatever 'in love' means …"
Instead, this couple handled themselves with the poise and judgement
of a gifted PR executive and an
experienced television presenter.

Was he ready for marriage now?
"If I'm not ready for it now, it's too
late, so yes", Edward said. "We are
the very best of friends, and that's
essential … and it also helps that
we happen to love each other as well
very much, and it's great. So we are
very happy at the moment and long
may it continue". Sophie revealed that their love
and friendship grew because "we share many
interests. We laugh a lot".

But what about joining the royal family?
"It is slightly nerve-wracking in many ways, but I
am ready for it now and I am fully aware of the
responsibilities and commitments".

*And her experience of working with the
press might help?* "Perhaps I am slightly better
geared up to second-guess what might happen",
said Sophie, before finally quashing suggestions
that they had lived together and that she had told
Edward to propose or lose her: "Contrary to popular opinion, we never lived together and I've never
issued any ultimatums".

They said they would like to be married at St
George's Chapel, Windsor ("It's just a wonderful
setting") and keep it "predominantly a family
wedding" and as low-key as possible. Edward
laughed: "I expect I'm going to be deeply
unpopular". Sophie agreed: "I think getting married

is a very personal thing, and naturally there is going
to be more interest in us than, obviously, with other
people, but it is a personal matter and it is a family
occasion". They laughed off a question about
starting a family. "Please, let's get through the first
stage!", said Edward, "One step at a time". Sophie
added: "We're not even married yet!"

*Would there be added pressures because of
other royal marriage breakdowns?* "Oh, somebody
had to bring that up, didn't they?", Edward smiled.
"More pressure? I don't know. I think if anybody's
going to get married, I hope that they think they are
going to get it right".

The path of true love

Edward and Sophie had no doubt that they *had* got
it right, but one question the prince avoided was
the big one of just why he had waited for so long.
For years, wedding news had seemed imminent
and, depending on which section of the authorit-
ative British Press you favoured, the royal romance

Above: A girl's best friend,
Sophie links arms with
Edward to show off her
modern-style triple-diamond
engagement ring to the
assembled photographers.

Above: An ambitious capricorn, 34-year-old Sophie spends the day at the office on her birthday. She arrives at her Mayfair headquarters carrying a beautiful bouquet of flowers – a gift from her fiancé?

was very certainly on, or most definitely off. Edward was said to have proposed, quietly bought Sophie an engagement ring and unofficially announced wedding plans to a small group of friends at an informal party – but stubbornly refused to let courtiers use the good news to divert constant media attention from his brothers' marital woes with Diana and Fergie. There were those stories about Sophie becoming increasingly impatient and claims that the romance was, in parlance known to the racing-mad royals, "all off at all meetings".

James Whitaker, *The Mirror*'s experienced royal commentator and columnist – and the man who wrote that front-page "It's off!" story for the tabloid in June 1994 – still believes there was a

> *"Speculation came when he took a lease on Bagshot Park, and when they were guests at other weddings"*

"cooling off" in the romance. He says: "Th[e] information came from a very senior and extremel[y] well-informed member of the royal household[.] they'd be absolutely astonished if they knew who[.] and about a year later someone equally in the kno[w] told me: 'You wer[e] absolutely right. The[y] *did* stop seeing eac[h] other for some time['.] But Sophie never men[t]tioned that story to m[e] when we met at recep[t]tions or racing at Roya[l] Ascot. She was ver[y] sweet and a good sport and even helped m[e] with a 'celebrity bet' we ran, nominating th[e] Macmillan Nurses as her chosen charity".

Still, though, the couple were saying nothin[g] about their plans, as Whitaker discovered when two years later, he found them far from the glamou[r] of London receptions and Royal Ascot. "It was that very hot summer of 1996", he remembers, "and I was covering the royal family's annual cruise around the Western Isles of Scotland. I'd yomped across miles of moorland and was having a little rest, looking down on where *Britannia* was moored in one of the creeks near Cape Wrath. Suddenly, I looked up and there were Edward and Sophie, out for a walk. It was a hell of a shock and I don't know who was more surprised, them or me. Sophie smiled, but didn't say a word, and Edward asked what I was doing there. After I explained, I asked when they were planning to marry. He said it was none of my business and off they went. He still wasn't committing himself".

Fresh speculation came some time afterwards when Edward took a lease on Bagshot Park and, inevitably, when the couple were guests at other weddings it was seen as a dress rehearsal for their own. Never more so than at the marriage of Sophie's older brother David to horsewoman Zara Freeland at the parish church of Northiam, East Sussex, in September 1996.

Sophie, determined that it should be a day for the bride and her brother David – an insurance company executive and amateur racing commentator – wanted to keep out of the limelight. Predictably, though, photographers flocked to the event and zoomed in on her and Edward, as the prince was pictured for the first time with his future in-laws.

Not long afterwards, Christopher Rhys-Jones met up again with his former prep school pupil Nigel Dempster for lunch. "I found him the same as ever", says Dempster, "a very nice, ordinary middle-class man. We met as former pupil and teacher, not as a journalist and the father of a future royal bride, but after we laughed about what he'd taught me, the subject of Sophie's marriage came up, because obviously something was going to happen fairly soon. Chris was very concerned about having to pay for the reception.

"I felt very sorry for him, because when your daughter gets married the last thing you want is people saying that the bride's father is not paying his share. But Chris simply hasn't got that sort of cash and, as I say, he's a very ordinary man who's never aspired to be anything else, and hadn't even met the Queen until fairly recently. So I tried to reassure him and tell him not to worry, because there are precedents for royal weddings. I said:

'If Sophie was marrying anyone else, you wouldn't be inviting hundreds of people to St George's Chapel and a great reception at Windsor Castle, would you?' I advised him to just lie back and enjoy it, and he seemed a little happier".

The long courtship

But even then, there was still the question of *when* the wedding would be. Why was Edward waiting? Sophie's friend Brian MacLaurin says: "Some people claim Edward is indecisive – although I'm told he can be quite tough in business – but I believe the very opposite is the case. He is a cautious and very private man, and very protective of Sophie. My perception is that he waited a long time because he was very conscious of the impact the marriage would have on Sophie and her family.

Above: Sophie arrives at the church for her brother's wedding in 1996, with her father and Edward a few steps behind. The prince's appearance at the ceremony guaranteed that the family occasion would be covered by the Press.

A STATELY HOME

Bagshot Park, the newlyweds' mansion in the Surrey countryside

Above: Edward and Sophie's new home is a Victorian mansion, originally commissioned by the prince's great-great-great grandmother, Queen Victoria, for her favourite son.

Just days before their engagement was announced, Sophie Rhys-Jones drove through the wrought-iron gates of Bagshot Park, the magnificent home in which she and Edward will start their married life, and stared up at its imposing Portland stone and redbrick Gothic facade. It was covered in scaffolding, and inside a frantic race was going on to get it ready for the big day – and for a future the couple are hoping will be as colourful and fascinating as their old home's past.

Set in more than 80 acres of beautiful tree-filled Crown Estate land, the mansion is ideally situated for the couple, within easy reach of both London and Windsor. It was built on the instructions of Queen Victoria and completed in 1887 as a wedding present for her third and favourite son, Prince Arthur, Duke of Connaught, and his wife, Princess Louise of Prussia, who in 1879 were also married in St George's Chapel, at Windsor. Unlike Prince Edward, the Duke enjoyed a long and decorated military career, eventually becoming colonel-in-chief of many regiments. Both he and the Duchess were a popular couple who endowed a number of hospitals in the nearby military town of Aldershot, where many roads and buildings still bear the name of Connaught.

Bagshot Park, now worth between £8 and £10 million, was a family home for the Duke and Duchess and their three children (together with some 60 servants) and when the Duke died in 1942, at the age of 91, it was requisitioned by the army as a wing of the Military Staff College. After World War II, it was considered for use as a country retreat for Princess Elizabeth, who as Queen is now Edward's "landlord", but instead the house became a training centre for army chaplains. Defence cuts forced the army to move out in 1996, and the following year Edward took a 50-year lease on the property and began renovations said to be costing £2 million.

"We are going to have to scale the house down to a more manageable size", he said on acquiring his new home, "there are too many rooms". He plans to have nine bedrooms with ensuite bathrooms, five reception rooms and three staff flats, with designs by Mary Montagu, daughter of Lord Montagu of Beaulieu. "Sophie is very involved and has her own taste", said the designer, revealing that the finished house will look "classic, with a contemporary twist".

In July 1998, Edward moved his firm's headquarters to a large stable block half a mile from the main house. "He's always been first in the office and last out", says Ardent chairman Malcolm Cockren, "often working from 9 am until 9 pm. And when he and Sophie move to Bagshot Park he'll be there even more, because he'll be working from home". It's been suggested that Sophie's PR skills might be used to help the company, so will she soon be working alongside her new husband in the stable office? "I'd be delighted to work with Sophie", says Cockren, "but we have to remember that she has her own very successful PR company, and I think it's very important for her ongoing relationship with Edward that she is just as successful as he is, but in their own individual businesses".

Left and above:
The Duke and Duchess of Connaught, who enjoyed a happy marriage and family life within the gates of Bagshot Park.

Above: Bagshot's jewel is the Indian Room, lined with hand-carved sandalwood panels made by Indian craftsmen.

Above: Sophie stands on deck of the *Britannia* with the Queen, Prince Edward, Tim Laurence, Peter Phillips and Prince Charles. The long courtship gave Sophie time to become accustomed to her new role within a rather unique family.

He wanted to give them time to come to terms with it, and for Sophie to learn what her role would be. All those musings in the media about him not wanting to go ahead because of Diana, and all the rest going on in the royal family, may have been true initially.

"But I believe Edward's primary concern was that Sophie was happy in the environment in which she would have to live, and that her parents were comfortable and understood and accepted what it would mean to them, and the role their daughter would have to play. Nothing other than time creates that understanding, and if Edward had rushed in he'd have been accused of being bullheaded and reminded about the fate of his brothers' marriages. So he just can't win, and I have great sympathy for the man. But he and Sophie have a very successful relationship and I'm sure their marriage will be a great success too, not least because of Sophie's attitude and understanding. Like Edward, she has thought long and hard about this and she knows it's the right thing to do".

> *"He wanted to give Sophie time to learn what her role would be"*

At Ardent, Malcolm Cockren says: "The constantly put off the idea of getting engage because they wanted to get themselves sorted ou and be in the right frame of mind for it. They wer determined to be absolutely sure that this wa what they both wanted, to be together foreve and of course that Sophie's company was goin well and Ardent was well on the way befor they married. Sophie is a wonderful, thorough nice person, which wi endear her to a lot c people. She and Edwar know what's at stak with their marriage and how important i is as far as the public perception of the roya family is concerned, and I can't believe they won make it a great success".

Nigel Dempster says: "I think they delaye because they wanted to be certain they were doin the right thing – and I believe Sophie when she say he'd never proposed before – and the fact that the did wait so long must give a tremendous boost t the chances of this marriage succeeding. I thin they're on a winner. Sophie will fit in very well

She's tough and sensible and has seen how it works. She's in our business and she's in their business, so she's got a foot in both camps, and Edward is a hard-working guy determined to make his way in the world on his own talents".

Despite that "It's off!" story he wrote back in 1994, James Whitaker says: "I think they waited until they were certain this is what they wanted to do, and I'm sure their marriage will work well and last. For the royal family it's got to, because the consequences if it were to fail are too catastrophic to even think about. Sophie is very sensible and under control, and I'm sure she's studied closely what happened to Diana and Fergie and is absolutely determined that it won't happen to her".

Business as usual

The morning after their engagement announcement, the couple showed they planned to continue with their normal working lives. Edward was back at his Ardent desk and Sophie drove from Buckingham Palace, where they'd celebrated well into the night, to her company's Mayfair headquarters. Wearing an elegant taupe trouser suit (and that ring), she greeted photographers and well-wishers with smiles but, asked how she felt, confessed: "I'm thinking of joining Insomniacs International!".

Left: Always a girl to enjoy a sporting break, Sophie embarks on her first "official" holiday with Edward, on the slopes of St Moritz in Switzerland.

Below left: The day after the big announcement Sophie returns to work, besieged by photographers. Within four months' time, she would have her own bodyguard to accompany her.

Soon afterwards, Sophie faced the daunting experience of sharing her first "official" holiday with Edward and the international Press corps. On a brief break at the fashionable Swiss ski resort of St Moritz, they laughed and joked as the cameras clicked, and Sophie showed off her snowboarding skills. Soon, though, it was back to business again, which for Edward meant a whistlestop tour of America – and more controversy.

His six-day tour, arranged by a New York lecture agency and sponsored by the Northern Trust Bank, took him from Miami to Beverly Hills, where he was feted at dinner or "English high tea" before giving 50-minute illustrated talks to the bank's invited guests on Windsor Castle's restoration after the fire. It was from America that encouragement came in Ardent's early days, when they found it difficult to persuade any British broadcaster to work with them, and Edward feels at home in the States. In Britain, he says, "people are more nervous about appearing to be in any way sucking up", but in the US "they tend to accept you on your credentials and don't get too hung up about your background".

As usual, he was well received everywhere, but back home newspaper stories said his was a "rent-a-royal" tour and accused him of making £200,000 by selling royalty to rich Americans. Many guests, it was claimed, believed his lectures were to raise money for the castle restoration.

But Ardent chairman Malcolm Cockren says: "The situation is perfectly clear. Edward went out with the specific job of raising the profile of Ardent. It was a gruelling trip, with sometimes two talks a day and the money he made is part of Ardent's bottom-line. Nothing went into his own pocket, as has been suggested, and at no time did he represent that these were charity functions".

> *"Sophie had learned as a career girl how to look good on a limited budget"*

In early March, Edward and Sophie underlined their wish to keep the wedding "a family affair", rather than a state occasion. They announced that they had chosen not to be married by the Archbishop of Canterbury – who usually officiates at royal marriage ceremonies – but by the Bishop of Norwich, the Right Rev. Peter Nott, who regularly conducts services for the royal family at Sandringham. And it was to be a "Continental-style" evening wedding with the service starting at 5 pm – posing for female guests the perennial problem of what to wear. A glamorous evening dress for the reception might display bare arms or cleavage, which would be highly unsuitable in church. One answer, from fashion experts: take a pashmina shawl or cashmere cardigan.

Sophie's style

For Sophie, there were more problems to face as she came to terms with her new role. Far from there being limited interest in the royal bride-to-be, as some had predicted, it increased massively, with almost daily newspaper stories and pictures about what she was doing – watching the Wales versus Ireland rugby game at Wembley, partnering the prince in a challenge golf match with Princess Anne and her husband, or out riding with the Queen in Windsor Great Park.

When Sophie was photographed leaving London's Hale Clinic, an exclusive alternative therapy centre close to Harley Street, it was claimed that she had been having acupuncture sessions with pregnancy expert Zita West, as part of plans for starting a family. But Buckingham Palace quashed that suggestion as "absolute rubbish". The truth was that for three years Sophie had been attending the clinic – once used by the Princess of Wales when she suffered back problems – for general acupuncture therapy, which was part of the centre's holistic techniques. A friend of Zita West's explained: "Sophie puts great faith in the ancient Chinese art, and Zita treats her for her general well-being, to help her cope with the strains and stresses of her high-profile public life". And stories that the couple planned to start a family soon after their wedding were pure speculation, said the Palace. "We are not privy to their private thoughts – nobody is".

Sophie was also said to be slimming and, allegedly upset at looking too big-hipped in her engagement-day photographs, was determined to trim down for the big day. And when she was pictured in April walking to Easter Service at St George's Chapel with Princess Anne's 17-year-old daughter, Zara, she looked to be succeeding.

Fashion pundits who had avidly analysed every detail of the late Princess of Wales's wardrobe, now switched their attention to Sophie, noting on that occasion her new "royal look" of a chic black suit with knee-length skirt and gold button detail on the jacket. But Sophie was determined not to be compared to Diana – so much that she reportedly informed the Queen she did not want the title of princess, because it would bring even more comparisons between the two of them. A friend was reported as saying: "Sophie feels the continued references and pictures comparing her to Diana do nothing at all to further her cause or help the royal family".

Opposite, top: Sophie shares a joke with Edward's niece, Zara Phillips, on the way to Easter Service at St George's Chapel. Her next rendezvous at the chapel would be on June 19.

Opposite, bottom: Sophie shows she can look as glamorous as any model, in a low-cut evening dress. As her royal role demands, she now splashes out on more designer outfits.

Above, right: As part of her public-profile grooming, Sophie has a top hairstylist, Andrew Collinge (pictured), to tend to her blonde tresses.

But while Diana was a international fashion icon – and with the pick of the best designers could pay anything from £2,000 to £15,000 for a dress – Sophie had learned as a career girl how to look good on a limited budget, seldom paying more than £250 for an outfit. And though she expanded her wardrobe for her royal role, she was largely sticking to safe and sensible suits.

Even her father's style was being analysed: one "royal expert" claimed that when Christopher and Mary Rhys-Jones had posed for photographers on the engagement day, he'd worn a favourite powder-blue sweater only after receiving advice from Buckingham Palace. After which, Adam Helliker reported in his *Sunday Telegraph* column: "Mr R-J has been joking that he can now only start dressing in the mornings once he has been sent a daily fax of sartorial instructions from courtiers".

As the wedding day approached, a host of Sophie "lookalikes" appeared on the lists of model agencies around Britain, available to bring a touch of phony royal glamour to commercial events. Another famous "Sophie double" in public perception was Jill Dando, the television presenter gunned down by a mystery assassin outside her London home at the end of April. She and Sophie had laughed about the comparison, become good friends and planned to swap wedding invitations – the TV girl was also due to married in the summer – and when she was murdered, Sophie joined many millions who mourned her. "I am deeply upset to hear this terrible news", she said.

Soon afterwards, amid heightened police security for public figures, Sophie was told she must learn to live with the "shadow" that has followed Edward all his life – an armed guard. Originally she had insisted, like Princess Diana, that she didn't want a bodyguard, and would often walk from Buckingham Palace across Green Park to her office. But after her friend's murder she was accompanied everywhere by an armed detective.

The big day approaches

Elsewhere there was happier news: at the Chelsea Flower Show the Queen was given a preview of the flowers chosen by Sophie for her wedding – a new variety of tall lilies, called "Crusader", nurtured by 57-year-old horticulturist Peter Smith at his nurseries near Pulborough, in West Sussex. Mr Smith, who also supplied flowers for the weddings of Charles and Andrew, was delighted to have been chosen again: "It is a small tradition I was very keen to continue", he said. "It is a great honour".

And at the Peter Jones China headquarters in Wakefield, West Yorkshire, they were producing commemorative mugs, beakers, paperweights and crystal bowls to mark the couple's engagement and marriage. "They are selling very well to our customers all over the world", said company director Daphne Jones.

Mainly, though the attention stayed on Sophie. There were more pictures when she attended other people's marriage services, including that of her wedding dress designer, Samantha Shaw, in May – a day after publication of that topless picture of

Sophie with Chris Tarrant had caused such a huge storm. On the day the picture was published, the shocked and "betrayed" Sophie had stayed out of sight at Buckingham Palace, from where she'd telephoned the bride and offered to stay away from the wedding at London's Chelsea Old Church, so not as to overshadow her friend's big day.

But Miss Shaw and her groom, City banker David Keswick, would not hear of it. So Sophie, after what were called "the worst 48 hours in her life", put on a brave face and turned up to face the cameras, looking stunning in a lilac coat-dress and wide-brimmed navy blue hat. Edward could not make it – he was said to be "detained at work" – but another guest, Prince Charles's long-standing companion Camilla Parker Bowles, *was* at the wedding. It was the first time she and Sophie had

Right: Sophie, unescorted by the prince, arrives at Chelsea Old Church for the marriage of her wedding dress designer, Samantha Shaw. The two women became firm friends over the many months of secret fittings for Sophie's bridal gown.

attended the same public event, but royal-watchers noted: "Neither woman appeared to greet each other".

A week later, at the beginning of June, Sophie hit the front pages again when she arrived at the wedding of her PR colleague Tania Wossman in Mayfair, London, wearing the *same hat* with its pink floral cluster. "Sophie's wedding hat trick", said one headline.

Next day, she was headline news again when *The Sun* issued another apology about the topless picture, was strongly condemned by the Press Complaints Commission for its "reprehensible" conduct – and lost the valuable sponsorship of the hit TV quiz show *Who Wants To Be A Millionaire?*, hosted by Chris Tarrant. "Chris wanted nothing to do with them", said an ITV spokesman. In view of the second apology, Edward and Sophie announced they would not pursue the complaint against the newspaper. "They now wish to put this issue behind them", said a Palace statement, "and concentrate on preparing for their wedding".

In May, newspapers discovered the *first* wedding picture of Sophie – when she played Cinderella in a flowing white dress. The snapshot was taken with other members of her dancing class, in June 1974, at St Andrew's Church annual garden party in Paddock Wood, Kent. Their teacher, Jane Bowerman, remembered: "Sophie was not the most talented dancer, but she was certainly one of the prettiest. She had this long blonde hair and the sweetest smile – so we decided she was perfect for our Cinderella. She looked absolutely lovely".

Final preparations …

Sophie, meanwhile, became increasingly busy with wedding preparations. She was photographed at the launch of a new diamond collection by jewellers Asprey & Garrard, and proudly wore the engagement ring they'd made for her. Just a few days later she was back there privately, trying on her wedding ring. She was also overseeing final work at Bagshot Park, future home for the newlyweds and their handful of staff – the prince's long-time valet Brian Osborne, a cook, and a secretary-and-dresser for Sophie. There was the all-important wedding list to sort out as well. Their gift list was placed at Thomas Goode, the upmarket store in London's Mayfair, with items ranging, as one report put it, 'from a modest £15 for a tennis net accessory to the mind-bogglingly dear".

Among their chosen items was a teapot crafted in silver for £8,800, with matching silver hot milk and water jugs at £10,000 each, a small milk jug for £3,925, a sugar sifter for £6,135 and a tea-strainer at £3,110, to complete the tea service. They also wanted a 26-piece fine bone china dinner service featuring their initials and a coronet (£13,580), a harlequin-design coffee set (with cups at £85 each) and similar tea cups (£108 each). For glassware, they chose Cumbria Crystal vintage champagne, claret, goblet and port glasses (around £1,000 for a set of 24) and to serve the wine, three silver jugs (£545 each). There was also a £1,178 Wedgwood dinner service and a sterling silver cutlery set for £9,000. For those guests on restricted budgets, there was a choice of more modestly priced gifts: a pair of tea tables (£125 each); two teak coffee tables (£190 each); Japanese lamps (£180 a pair); a badminton set (£160); souffle dishes (£61 each); or perhaps just a nice tree to grace the grounds of Bagshot Park (various prices).

The good news in the run-up to the big day, though, came when the couple decided to invite 8,000 members of the public to what they'd originally intended to be a "family wedding". Buckingham Palace said people would be invited to apply for tickets, and the lucky 8,000 would be allowed to take prime spots outside St George's Chapel to see the couple arrive and depart.

Edward Windsor and his bride were to have a "People's Wedding" after all.

Above: The elegant Castle of Mey china tea service, from Edward and Sophie's wedding list at Thomas Goode. With the finest silver, crystal and china, the couple will be able to entertain in grand style.

Chapter Eight

THE BIG DAY

The crowds gather in the sunshine for the last royal wedding of the Millennium

At last the big day arrived, and with it an early surprise. The Queen, it was announced, had decided that her youngest son, seventh in line to the throne, should be known as the Earl of Wessex and Viscount Severn, making his bride the Countess of Wessex.

As constitutional experts argued its significance, crowds gathered in the historic old town of Windsor from early morning for a glimpse of the bride and her dress. They were not disappointed. Sophie Rhys-Jones looked as any bride should. Stunning. Radiant. Beautiful.

Her wedding – unique in the annals of royal marriages – went off perfectly, with just one small hitch when Edward had trouble getting the ring on her finger. But after that it was plain sailing, with a ride through the town and cheering crowds, a friendly family reception and an emotional send-off as they left on honeymoon and their new life together.

"It was a very emotional goodbye", said one who saw them off. "They are obviously so very much in love".

Left: Newly created Earl and Countess, and newly married. Edward and Sophie exchange a loving look after the service in the chapel. They are flanked by the bridesmaids and pages that so charmed the crowds in their matching outfits designed by Samantha Shaw.

"They gave a sure sign that the marriage would flourish"

The eyes said it all. Everyone agreed on that afterwards. It was that long and lingering look straight into each other's eyes as they exchanged their sacred marriage vows which told their families and friends, and the watching world, that this was the most serious venture of their lives, and one they were determined should and would succeed.

From a couple known for their love of laughter, which helped bring them close together in the first place, and which threatened to break out at other, less serious, moments of the marriage ceremony, there was not a hint, a flicker, even a slight suggestion of a smile. Just that solemn, almost unblinking, determined near-stare into each other's eyes which told everything about the love and loyalty and total commitment of Prince Edward and Sophie Rhys-Jones.

For the Queen and her husband Philip, watching intently close by, it was as sure a sign as any that this marriage, of their youngest son, would flourish where those of their other children had so publicly floundered and failed. For Edward's brothers, Charles and Andrew, standing beside him as his supporters – royalty's version of the best man role – it was a grim reminder of what might have been in their own wrecked marriages.

For Sophie's parents, Christopher and Mary Rhys-Jones, it was a strong signal that their only daughter, always a solid and sensible middle-class girl who knows her own mind, would fit almost effortlessly into her new role with the royal family. And for the wider world it was confirmation enough that this, surely, was at last a royal marriage which could end with a "happily ever after".

That was the big, important difference. But there were many others: it was the first royal wedding of recent years without pomp and pageantry, bands and military ballyhoo, and largely a bit of a family do. It was the first at which friends

"A difficult decision over what style to wear"

and colleagues of the couple were on an equal footing with European royalty, and politicians were not invited – although British Premier Tony Blair sent his good wishes and said he was sure they'd be "tremendously happy" together. And, in keeping with the bride and groom's modern outlook on life, it was the first evening, "Continental-style" wedding, posing for women guests with the perennial problem of what to wear, the additional difficulty of managing to look modestly sedate at the service and glamorous and chic at the reception immediately afterwards.

Some were doubtless still pondering the problem when the first crowds began to gather in the historic streets around Windsor Castle at 6am and the lucky 8,000 chosen by ballot to take "ringside seats" outside St George's Chapel were finding their places. They brought "Good Luck!" banners and balloons and flags and picnic hampers and flasks of tea, which has sustained the British through innumerable crises. They brought portable radios and TV sets so as not to miss a moment of

Right: Dedicated royal watcher William Willis bags a prime spot on Castle Hill to view the proceedings. He would be joined by 30,000 spectators in Windsor and 200 million TV viewers around the world.

Left: Edward walks from the castle to the chapel with his brotherly supporters (best men) Prince Charles and Prince Andrew. Traditionally it's part of the best man's job to keep the groom calm and collected before the service – and Andrew seems to be doing a fine job by keeping Edward's mind on lighter matters. But Charles? He seems to be somewhat pre-occupied . . . perhaps he's worried about losing the two rings in his pocket!

Below: After leaving their cars in Long Park nearby, most of the 550 guests were ferried through the town to the chapel. For some of these distinguished guests, it must have been their first-ever trip on a bus!

the day's events, and newspapers packed with pictures and every last detail about "Ed and Soph".

They were joined by visitors from all around the world – from America and Canada, Australia, Germany, France and Japan and elsewhere – and all had one thing in common: they were prepared to wait all day to see and say they'd been at this last Royal Wedding of the Twentieth Century.

The world watches

As an estimated 30,000 gathered, they were surrounded by the vans and cameras, cables and other paraphernalia of broadcasters who would beam the proceedings to an estimated audience of more than 200 million around the globe. Among the first of them there was the BBC's Michael Buerk, who was presenting the wedding programme with Sue Barker, the former tennis star whose enforced absence at a photo-shoot had brought Sophie and Edward together. Strolling

Left: Ruthie Henshall and John Gordon Sinclair were just two of the representatives from the world of showbiz on the guest list. She had been linked romantically with Edward before he met Sophie. But the two remain firmest of friends.

Below: Edward's proud parents linger just inside the chapel before the service, with the Rt Rev. Peter Nott, Bishop of Norwich.

around the Castle precincts, Buerk came across Prince Edward. "And *he* wished *me* luck!", the laughing broadcaster told his huge audience later.

For him, and other media men and women from around the world, there was soon a shock announcement to get their teeth into: Buckingham Palace revealed that the Queen had made Edward the Earl of Wessex and Viscount Severn, with his bride-to-be to become Her Royal Highness the Countess Wessex. The secondary title of Viscount Severn would pass as a courtesy title to their eldest son. And Edward would also be given the Dukedom of Edinburgh after the death of the Queen and her husband.

For months there had been speculation about what title, if any, Edward would be given. Sophie was said to have made it plain that she did not want to be called Princess or anything else – and even now, in her business life, will be known as Sophie Wessex. But the Queen's decision reflected her desire to modernize the monarchy, and to fulfil the

> ## "Sophie had always said that she wanted the wedding to be a family occasion"

wishes of the couple to live on the fringes of the royal family.

It did not please constitutional experts, most of whom had confidently predicted that Edward would be named Duke of Cambridge … or Sussex … or Connaught. The title of Earl, many pointed out, is usually given to a commoner marrying into the royal family – the Earl of Snowdon received his title when he married Princess Margaret – and the Wessex earldom has not been conferred since the 10th century. It was, some said, a slight to Edward that he had not been given a royal dukedom.

Historian Dr David Starkey declared: "I think this represents a very unusual compromise, and the Queen is very ill-advised to do it. We have just abolished the voting rights of the hereditary peers in the House of Lords, and to create another title is a step backwards – particularly when it is a title which has very little to do with the royal family".

He added: "The title itself is a total fiction. There is nowhere called Wessex. It belongs to the novels of Thomas Hardy. The title has not been used for 1,000 years. Is it the right way to celebrate

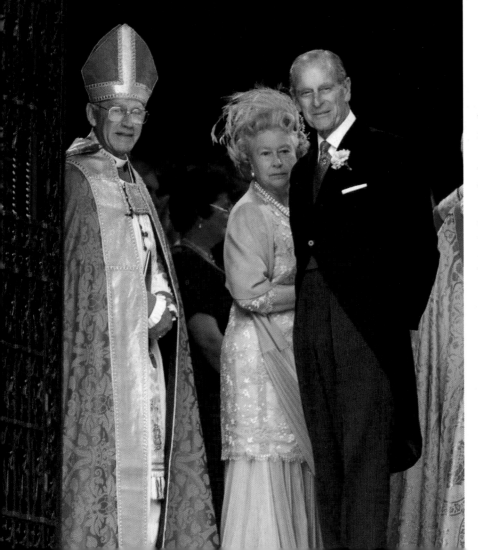

Henshall, with actor John Gordon Sinclair; former racing driving ace Jackie Stewart and his wife…

It was a great day for celebrity-spotting, and for seeing how women guests coped with that fashion problem. Most, it was agreed, handled it brilliantly, with shawls and jackets and cardigans which could be taken off for the reception. And largely they obeyed the specific "No Hats" request, which Edward explained in a TV interview with ITV's Sir Trevor McDonald screened before the ceremony: "It seemed to be simpler just to have the whole affair in basically evening wear", he said. "So the ladies didn't have to wear hats, and then there was never a problem of what they were going to do with them afterwards".

The ladies who ignored the request were mainly those of more mature years for whom a wedding without a new hat would be flying in the face of tradition, let alone fashion. Not least the Queen

Left: Lord Lloyd-Webber with his wife Mariane. He commented: "I love these occasions" – and certainly, for the crowd, watching the celebrities added a special ingredient to the day.

Below: Prince William and Prince Harry, impeccably turned out, leave the chapel after the 45-minute service.

the third millennium by going back to the first?"

Edward and Sophie, though, were obviously quite pleased with the Queen's decision – and the crowds waiting to see them couldn't give a duke's coronet about the constitutional argument, which went over their uncrowned heads. They waited patiently under darkening skies, praying that threatening rain wouldn't spoil Sophie's big day – and theirs. And their long wait was rewarded shortly before 4.30pm when the first of the mini-coaches brought the early arrivals among the 550 guests to St George's Chapel from picking-up points outside the Windsor Castle precincts.

Arriving in style!

People who hadn't been on a bus for years – if ever – started to arrive in them. There was the Sultan of Brunei – said to be a big stakeholder in Edward's Ardent TV company – with his family; Prince and Princess Michael of Kent; the broadcaster Sir David Frost; the prince's former boss Andrew Lloyd Webber; actor Anthony Andrews and his wife; Edward's good friend and old flame Ruthie

Right: Sir David Frost, eminent TV personality, clearly enjoying the happy occasion to the full.

Below: The Queen Mother's arrival was greeted with huge cheers from the crowd – these redoubled when she walked unaided, except for a stick, to the chapel.

Mother, who would be 99 years young a few weeks hence and who many cannot recall ever seeing without some stunning millinery concoction above her ever-present smile.

She was on her way from her home, Royal Lodge, Windsor – where she'd entertained Sophie and her parents and brother David overnight – as, at 4.46pm, the crowds caught their first glimpse of the bridegroom. He came strolling down to St George's Chapel with his brothers – he and Andrew in dark morning suits, Charles sporting an individual grey. "There are no rules for royal families", said one commentator. "They can wear what they want". At least there was a pocket for the rings, and Charles, like any best man, kept delving into it to make sure they were still there. They were.

Edward looked in jubilant mood, waving and smiling at the cheering crowds and saying "Thank you very much" all along the route to the chapel. Once there, the brothers mounted the West Steps in line, were welcomed by the Dean and, as the congregation rose to greet them, made their way down the rich royal-blue aisle carpet to the bookshop of the 700-year-old chapel to await the bride's arrival.

The generations together

Soon afterwards, at 4.40pm, there were more huge cheers as the Queen Mother (in another stunning hat) arrived at the Galilee Porch and walked with the aid of a stick to her place. For her daughter Princess Margaret, who badly burned her feet in a holiday accident, there was a far more discreet arrival, and she was pushed to her place in the chapel in a wheelchair.

Other royals, including Princess Anne, arrived in a fleet of three mini-buses. There were Charles's sons, the Princes William and Harry, and Edward's girls, Beatrice and Eugenie. There was, of course, no sign of their mother, Sarah Ferguson, who, like Prince Charles' companion Camilla Parker Bowles, was pointedly not invited. Fergie said publicly that

she was disappointed, and as her children arrived, she was said to have flown off to Italy to avoid all the fuss.

Even the children are used to public occasions, of course, but for one woman it was a nerve-wracking day. Mary Rhys-Jones, who arrived at the chapel 15 minutes before her daughter – and hatless, as instructed, had said she wasn't nervous "until someone asks me if I am". It had been bad enough when she and husband Christopher first heard that their daughter was dating Prince Edward: "It was the first time in my life that I have ever had a gin and tonic before 10 in the morning", he'd said then. But this was a far greater ordeal for both, and they faced it bravely.

A DREAM OF A DRESS

The wedding dress and the designer who created it

As Sophie stepped out of her Rolls-Royce in front of St George's Chapel, all eyes fell on her beautiful and elegant gown, created amid much secrecy by little-known London designer, Samantha Shaw.

A coup for the young designer, Shaw's name wasn't near the top of fashion pundits' lists of hopefuls when Sophie and Edward first revealed their wedding plans. Instead, the spotlight fell on another important man in Sophie's life – favourite designer Tomasz Starzewski. Immediately, there was speculation that he would design

her wedding gown, and during New York fashion week in February he unveiled some of his ideas for a bride's big day. As designers almost fell over themselves to dress the royal bride, Sophie was saying nothing. "Some have already sent in their ideas", she revealed, but I'm not going to tell anybody what the dress will be like. Not even my best friends".

Exquisite beading and trimmings

But the fashion experts got it all wrong: in April it was revealed that Sophie had chosen Samantha Shaw, a virtually unknown 30-year-old, to make the wedding dress of the year – and catapult her to the sort of prominence achieved by David and Elizabeth Emanuel, who made Princess Diana's fairytale dress, and Lindka Cierach, who produced Fergie's gown.

Miss Shaw's credentials are impeccable: she is part of the McAlpine building dynasty on her mother Valerie's side, and father Peter is a film producer whose credits include *Champions*. And just three weeks before Sophie's wedding, she was married herself, to David Keswick, banker son of Prince Charles's friends Sir Chips and Lady Keswick.

Samantha Shaw studied at the Paris Academy of Fashion, took a course in theatre and film costume design in London and worked as a designer's assistant, before setting up her own business in 1992. Soon word of her individual style – fastidious attention to detail and exquisite beading and trimmings – spread, and though never high-profile, she now numbers among her clients Liz Hurley, Caprice, Ivana Trump's daughter Ivanka, and Serena Linley, wife of the Queen's nephew Viscount Linley. Sophie had admired several Samantha Shaw creations, not least the gown of Isabella Norman at her 1998 wedding to Timothy Knatchbull, grandson of

the late Earl Mountbatten, before she approached the designer to make her own wedding dress.

With the commission agreed at an estimated £35,000, the very discreet designer and a handful of assistants quietly disappeared to a secret address to complete their most important project ever. "I think Samantha had a few worries about all the attention", a friend said, "but she's absolutely thrilled to be making Sophie's dress".

Although the dress will be copied by brides throughout the world, Sophie will be happy not to become a fashion icon like Princess Diana. "If she'd

wanted to be a trend-setter", a close friend said, "she'd have chosen something much more sensational than that neat and nice suit she wore to announce the engagement. Sophie doesn't want to be a highly photographed woman. She will very deliberately stay away from all that. Sophie just wants the privacy that Edward yearns".

Above: Supermodel Caprice and Christine Estrada wearing glamorous Samantha Shaw designs.

Opposite, main picture: Sophie's dress consists of a long, fitted, panelled coat with long sleeves and train; the fabric is hand-dyed silk organza and silk crepe. Pearls and crystal beading line the neck, sleeves and train.

Opposite, inset: Sophie ties a length of fabric around her waist to mimic her train, during a dress rehearsal for the wedding.

Left: Samantha Shaw, designer of Sophie's much-admired wedding dress.

Above: Sophie's diamond tiara came from the Queen's private collection; the black-and-white pearl necklace with gold rondels and matching earrings, were designed by Edward.

The first sight of him, and the bride, came as their car – the Queen's very best black, glass-topped Rolls Royce – came down from Royal Lodge, Windsor and the crowds strained to get a view of her and that dress. As always, it was not until the bride arrived at the church, just six minutes late, that her full glory was seen.

Perfect coordination

As Sophie emerged from the car at the West Door of St George's Chapel – which is steeped in history but has seen only three royal marriages this century – the crowds saw that her dress was soft and elegant and classical, in an oyster shade of silk crepe and organza, embroidered with 325,000 cut-glass beads and pearls. The corseted dress, with a V-neck, had a medieval feel, and her hand-dyed silk tulle veil was an inch longer than the train. It was only enhanced by a shimmering tiara, lent by the Queen, and Edward's present to his bride – a black-and-white pearl necklace with cross pendant and matching earrings.

It co-ordinated perfectly with the regal black-and-white theme of the bridesmaids and page-boys

– outfits which, it was remarked, looked like mini-versions of Knights of the Garter, whose traditional home is Windsor. It was the biggest day in the young lives of the two bridesmaids – eight-year-old Camilla, daughter of Edward's PR friend Abel Hadden, and Olivia, five-year-old daughter of Sophie's close friend Lindy Taylor. And for the pageboys – Harry Warburton, five-year-old son of Edward's personal assistant Sarah, and Felix, the seven-year-old son of the couple's friends Julian and Lucinda Sowerbutts.

"The dress was soft and elegant and classical, in an oyster shade of silk crepe and organza"

They waited patiently as Sophie's dress designer, Samantha Shaw, helped her arrange the gown and the veil blowing in the breeze. Then Christopher Rhys-Jones, carrying the bride's bouquet of garden roses, lily of the valley, freesias and stephanotis in ivory shades, took her arm and guided her slowly up the 22 steps she was dreading to face. Together, they did it faultlessly, and as her arrival was heralded by the specially-composed "Fanfare for Sophie", they prepared for another daunting walk – up that royal-blue aisle carpet. Again they did it perfectly, with Chris Rhys-Jones – who was celebrating his birthday as well as all this –

Left: Crowds of eager onlookers spill onto the aptly named Long Walk that leads from the castle to the Copper Horse as the bride's car makes its sedate way to the chapel.

Opposite: Dress designer Samantha Shaw and Sophie's father make final adjustments to the bride's train before she ascends the steps to the chapel.

Below: Chris Rhys-Jones arrives with the bride. It was truly a special day for him: his daughter's wedding and his own birthday.

effortlessly guiding his daughter through the chapel which has seen so much British history and was decorated today with 10,000 blooms.

All 550 pairs of eyes were on them – with, unusually, their seats facing outwards to the aisle – and on either side of the quire, three rows of wooden stalls usually reserved for Knights of the Garter, were packed with the couple's closest relatives and friends. Above the stalls hung the colourful banner of each Knight, with their helmets and crests below.

Royals and members of the Rhys-Jones family sat in the inner-sanctum of St George's Chapel for a close-up view of Edward and Sophie's marriage ceremony.

Sophie's parents, Christopher and Mary Rhys-Jones, her brother David and his wife Zara sat on the left, opposite the Queen, Queen Mother, Prince of Wales, Duke of Edinburgh, Princess Margaret and Duke of York closest to the altar in the chapel's quire.

When the once-wayward Marina Ogilvy entered St George's Chapel, her presence at the wedding signified a return to the royal fold. Marina, 32, who

Right: Chris Rhys-Jones, carrying the bride's bouquet, guides his daughter slowly and carefully up the 22 steps to the chapel.

Opposite: Princess Anne, Sophie's brother David, and Zara Phillips (behind her mother).

Below: The Bishop of Norwich greets the bride as the bridesmaids and pages take position. Chris Rhys-Jones helps with the final touches to the train.

ended her stormy, seven-year marriage to photographer Paul Mowatt in 1997, took her wedding seat, in the Garter Knights' stalls, in the midst of senior royals. It was her highest-profile royal occasion since the divorce. Marina and Paul have an eight-year-old daughter, Zenouska, and five-year-old son, Christian.

Edward and his brothers had moved to their places, with Charles again digging into his waistcoat pocket to check that the rings were still there. They were. Edward, looking a little nervous for the first time, fingered the 18-carat hunter pocket watch Sophie had given him as a wedding present. His bride-to-be looked straight ahead as she came down the aisle and Edward, spotting her for the first time, seemed frozen with nerves. In a break with tradition, the couple met in the nave of the Chapel, rather than at the altar, which was obscured from most of the guests.

Both looked straight ahead as the Bishop of Norwich, the Rt Rev. Peter Nott, began the service. Then, as they stood at the sanctuary step for the first hymn, their sense of humour came through and they both smiled. Edward gave her a huge and supposedly secret wink – the fact that it was seen by more than 200 million people around the world didn't seem to matter.

The look of love

Having a hymn to sing seemed to settle their nerves and Edward sang it lustily, with Sophie trying to sing along. But soon it was over and it was time for them to exchange vows. It was then that their eyes locked on each other, unwavering, determined, purposeful, totally aware of what they were saying. Unlike Diana Spencer, who famously got her new husband's Christian names muddled up, Sophie Rhys-Jones was word-perfect and spoke audibly and sincerely. She promised, as the world knows, to obey, which she has explained means having trust in your partner. Edward's voice was also clear and firm as he said: "I will". Even the noise of Heathrow jets screaming overhead could not block out their meaning, and the crowds outside heard those words broadcast, and cheered – as they did again later when the couple were finally pronounced man and wife.

There was, though, one heart-stopping moment, which those outside could not see, which threatened to mar the otherwise-faultless proceedings. It came as Edward tried to slide the plain wedding band of Welsh gold on to Sophie's ring finger – and struggled to get it over her knuckle. It took a little time, but eventually he succeeded. Royal jeweller David Thomas said later that his heart missed a beat when it happened. "It is not unusual for this to happen", he added. "It was certainly a bit tight and just like everyone else my heart missed a beat. It was down to nerves, and heat inside the chapel, which swelled Sophie's finger".

"It was down to nerves, and heat inside the chapel, which swelled Sophie's finger"

In contrast, Sophie slid her ring on to Edward's little finger in one smooth action. But why the little finger and not the wedding finger? Had she got it wrong? Royal watchers were puzzled by the couple's choice to have the ring on Edward's "wrong" finger, next to the signet ring bearing his crest. But aides said it was traditional for a royal prince to wear a ring on his signet finger. And Edward had decided to do things differently from ordinary couples.

After the drama the couple bowed their heads as they were pronounced man and wife – and Sophie Rhys-Jones of Homestead Farmhouse, Brenchley,

Opposite: All 550 pairs of eyes fix on the beautiful bride as Sophie and her father walk up the aisle.

Below: The bride and groom exchange nervous smiles as the Bishop begins the service.

Right: A difficult moment as Edward struggles to fit the wedding ring onto his bride's finger.

ent, became the Countess of Wessex. Her brother, avid, read the Lesson taken from the First Letter f John, chapter four, verses 7-11, and then the ouple knelt on cushions before the Dean of Vindsor and recited, along with the congregation, he Lord's Prayer.

Prayers followed, in which the Dean referred to ophie as "being loving, amiable and faithful to her usband". Then the 23 choristers broke into song or the first time with a Latin anthem, "When There s Charity and Love There is God". There was a lessing from the Bishop. A fanfare broke the ilence and everyone stood for the last hymn. And s they sang "Let All The World In Every Corner ing, My God and King", Edward took his new vife's hand gently in his and they walked together o the ambulatory to sign the registers.

It was there, accompanied by the Queen and rince Philip and Christopher and Mary Rhys-

Right: The blessing, and a relieved smile: the Earl and Countess of Wessex are finally man and wife.

Below: The bride curtsies and the groom bows; they have made their vows to each other, and their new life together has begun.

Jones, that the groom kissed his bride – a very private occasion and not one for public consumption. The serious business over, they emerged again among the congregation in the chapel – and now there were wide, beaming smiles from Edward and Sophie for their relatives and friends as they walked slowly down the aisle to face the outside world. Everyone else was smiling, too. The Queen looked happier than many have seen her for some time, smiling broadly as she watched the couple leave. And Sophie's parents looked equally happy – relieved that it was all over.

"She looked gorgeous all day … She's a real poppet"

Outside, huge cheers greeted the appearance of the couple on the chapel steps. But calls for "A kiss!" went unheard. They stayed only briefly, before climbing into Ascot landaus – used at the race meeting during the week – for the drive through Windsor back to their reception. Again they were given a rousing welcome from people who'd been on these streets since early morning. Plainly very happy and smiling at the public reaction, they waved and pointed and mouthed "Thank you's" at those who shouted "Good luck!"

Above: Edward helps his new bride down the steps to their waiting carriage. There were calls for a kiss from the waiting crowd – but they had already kissed in the privacy of the chapel's ambulatory.

Opposite: The couple emerge from the chapel and exchange tender looks. They appear truly relaxed for the first time!

Above: The magnificent 500-year-old St George's Chapel, where generations of the royal family have attended services.

Left: The main chapel entrance through the west door. The west front features the third-largest stained-glass window in England, dating from the 1500s.

GOING TO THE CHAPEL

The long and distinguished history of St George's Chapel

St George's Chapel at Windsor Castle is a magnificent example of typically English late-medieval Gothic architecture, and it was its glory, setting and "peaceful atmosphere" as well as being "somewhere slightly different", that made Edward and Sophie choose it for their marriage.

The chapel is one of a number of the royal family's personal places of worship which include Crathie Church at Balmoral and St Mary Magdalene at Sandringham. St George's is, however, unrivalled amongst them, steeped in 500 years of history at the very heart of the monarchy.

Founded in 1070 as a formidable fortress beside the River Thames, Windsor Castle has been home to English monarchs from the time of William the Conqueror. Here in 1110 Henry I first held court at "the New Windsor", and in 1348 Edward III established the Order of the Garter, Britain's most senior order of chivalry, comprising only the sovereign, immediate family members and a small number of knights

npanion. Their motto *honi soit qui
l y pense* (the shame be his who
nks badly of it) came, it's said, from
ward, as he tied a garter, dropped by
dy, to his own leg.

Foundations of history

ward IV commissioned the building
the chapel in 1475, but work was
ly completed after his death, over a
iod of 50 years and the reigns of
ee kings. Since the 15th century,
George's has become the spiritual
me of the Order of the Garter, where
banners, helmets and crests of the
ights hang above the choir stalls. The
een presides over a spectacular
emony each year, when she and the
er knights parade through the castle
cincts to the chapel, wearing the
wing velvet robes and white-plumed
s of the order.

Edward and Sophie's marriage
vice was the latest in a long line of
al weddings to take place at the
apel, though it was the first time in
r a century that the child of a
ereign had married there. The last
al wedding at St George's was of
dy Helen Windsor, daughter of the
Duke and Duchess of Kent, to art dealer
Tim Taylor in 1992, but the most
glorious came when Princess Alexandra
of Denmark, called "the loveliest
Princess in Europe", married the Prince
of Wales on March 10, 1863.

Alexandra was just 18, and "pale
and plainly trembling" in a crinoline
profusion of Honiton lace, as she
exchanged vows with the future King
Edward VII. Like Sophie, who has loved
the chapel's atmosphere since first
attending services with the royal family,
Alexandra knew she was at the very
heart of English history, the last resting
place of ten kings, including Henry VIII
and Charles I.

For Queen Victoria, her son's
marriage was a bitter-sweet occasion.
Not long widowed, she ordered that no-
one see her overwhelming grief, and an
elaborate scheme was devised to meet
her wishes. The Queen walked to the
North Terrace and through a private
garden into the deanery. From its
drawing-room, Victoria – dressed
completely in black – stepped onto the
cloister's leaded roof, where a pathway
had been built to a door beside the
Great East Window. That brought her
into the Royal Closet, designed by Henry
VIII for his first wife, Catherine of
Aragon, to watch the Garter ceremonies
at the High Altar below.

There, almost hidden by heavy blue
velvet curtains, "the widow of Windsor"
saw her son married. Afterwards, she
left by the same route, and as the
wedding celebrations began, went to
Frogmore in Windsor Park to pray at the
tomb of Albert – the man who, as she
wrote on the day after her own wedding,
had made her "the happiest, happiest
Being" that ever existed.

Left: Henry III's doorway, found in the
ambulatory, was the original west door and
the intricate iron scrollwork bears the name
of its maker, Gilbertus.

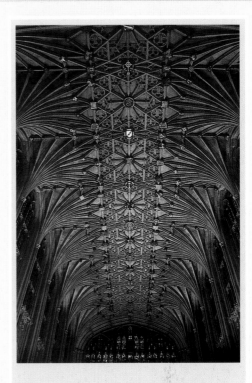

Above: The vaulted ceiling of the nave is an
exquisite example of Perpendicular Gothic, a
particularly English style, which challenged the
engineering skills of the medieval stonemasons.

Below: A view of the choir, looking west
towards the sovereign's stall. The banners of
the present knights companion of the Order of
the Garter hang above the stalls.

At the reception, in Windsor Castle's S[t] George's Hall, guests were greeted by music from a string quartet from the National Youth Orchestra o[f] Scotland, who Edward actively supports. They wer[e] served with canapés and champagne before bein[g] ushered through for the self-service dinne[r] reception at 8pm. But, in keeping with th[e] unconventional style of the whole wedding, the[y] had to wait until the speeches and toasts wer[e] made, and the cake cut, before they got their mea[l].

"The cake was amazing", said one guest. "It wa[s] decorated with lots of daffodils in honour o[f] Sophie's Welsh ancestry, and some tennis racquet[s] to mark how they met".

First to speak was Edward himself, who toaste[d] the Queen on behalf of himself and "my wife" which drew cheers from the guests. Sophie's fathe[r] then toasted his daughter and new son-in-law. B[y] now, said one guest, Christopher Rhys-Jones ha[d] lost any earlier nerves. "He seemed to be enjoyin[g] every minute of it". Afterwards, there were toasts t[o] the bridesmaids and pages from Charles an[d] Andrew. And a fanfare from the Royal Marines ban[d] signalled the cutting of the cake – all four feet an[d] four tiers of it – to applause from the guests[.] Throughout it all, Edward and Sophie mingled wit[h] their relatives and friends, stopping at each grou[p] to share stories and laughs.

A royal banquet

When they moved to the self-service buffet, laid o[ut] in the magnificent surroundings of the recentl[y] restored St George's Hall after the disastrous fire o[f] 1992, guests could choose from a menu of smoke[d] haddock coulibiac, beef stroganoff and a selectio[n] of vegetables and salads, followed by fres[h] raspberries prepared by the royal kitchens an[d] chosen by the Queen's chef Lionel Mann.

Then it was on to the evening entertainmen[t] and Sophie and Edward took to the dance floor a[s] man and wife, dancing to a jazz band and musi[c] from Sting, Scott Joplin and a medley of Sixtie[s] songs, including The Beatles and The Rollin[g] Stones. The Royal Marines band also provide[d] music, playing more traditional songs befor[e] donning sunglasses and bursting into a Blue[s] Brothers routine.

One guest, Duncan Bullivant, a friend o[f] Edward's from his Gordonstoun schooldays, sai[d] later that the newlyweds enjoyed themselve[s] immensely: "They danced to lots of songs

Above: Making their way to the reception, the Duchess of Gloucester (far right) with her daughters, Prince Michael of Kent (second from left) with son Lord Frederick (far left) and daughter Lady Gabriella (behind).

Right: Princess Eugenie, Prince William and Prince Harry look on as the public welcomes another member to the royal family.

Opposite: Her Majesty the Queen laughs with joy after the marriage service of her youngest son, with high hopes that this will be a happy union.

Above: The family watch as the happy couple prepare to ride to the reception in an Ascot landau. The carriage, with painted basketweave sides, is normally used by the Queen and her guests during Royal Ascot.

including 'Delilah' by Tom Jones and 'YMCA' by The Village People". His friend Clare Chance, added: "They were very at ease and extremely happy. It was a very personal and relaxed affair".

It had been a long day, and the newlyweds were tiring. Sophie, who had by now changed into a cream-coloured suit, and Edward in a dark suit, decided to call it a day at five minutes past midnight. They departed in a Rolls Royce, to which someone – brother Andrew was the main suspect – had tied red heart-shaped balloons. And as the limousine pulled out of Windsor's Long Walk, they disappeared to be on their own. Very few knew their honeymoon destination – although speculation was that they would start it in the privacy of Balmoral, the Queen's Highland estate in Scotland, before going somewhere warm.

One special guest at the wedding and reception was Malcolm Cockren, Prince Edward's friend, and chairman at Ardent, who has helped greatly with the preparation of this book. He was invited with

> *"They were very at ease and extremely happy. It was a very personal and relaxed affair"*

his wife, Linda, and the day afterwards he told me: "It was a very special day for both of us. One we will never ever forget.

"I rang Edward on the previous evening, to wish him well, and he sounded in great form. He had just been at the wedding rehearsal with Sophie and it had all gone very well. While he was there he looked over the TV cameras and the way the BBC were planning to cover the service – something as a TV man he was very obviously interested in – and was very happy indeed. He said: 'The BBC have done a tremendous job, and I couldn't be more happy with them'. After he knew that would go well, I think everything just slotted into place for him and for Sophie.

"She looked gorgeous all day yesterday. She's a real poppet. And she and Edward are very obviously so happy together. The wedding went off wonderfully well, and the reception was very special. It was just like a private family wedding. Every member of the royal family was relaxed and happy, and made the guests feel the same way too. It was a delightful evening in every way, and it all went off perfectly. Every member of the family spent the entire evening walking around talking to everybody. It was all so nice and natural.

"I had only about two minutes chatting with Edward and about three minutes with Sophie, because of course everyone wanted to talk to them and congratulate them, and I see them very regularly. But they were both bubbling and happy and plainly delighted that it had all gone off so very well".

Malcolm Cockren added: "It was quite an emotional occasion, and for me by far and away the most emotional part was at the end of the whole day, in the private courtyard at Windsor, just after midnight when they left in the glass-roofed Rolls Royce, with the castle illuminated and the royal standard flying over it.

"About 50 of us lined the route it would take before it went through the gateway and they were beaming all over their faces and obviously couldn't have been happier. They drove out very slowly, with a lone Scottish piper leading the car, and it was wonderful to see. I don't mind admitting I felt very emotional as they left. It had been the most perfect day for them. And for us".

And, indeed, for the world. Next day, the tabloid *New York Post*'s Sunday edition carried a picture of the newlyweds across the front page under the headline "Royal Bliss". Its coverage described it as a "traditional ceremony long on modern fairy-tale romance and refreshingly short on stuffy royal pomp", even though the paper recognized that it "was not as breathlessly anticipated as the union between Prince Charles and Lady Diana, or even Prince Andrew's marriage to . . . Sarah Ferguson".

Breaking the mould for the new millennium?

The Chicago Tribune carried extensive coverage of the wedding on its website, including a separate photo file of pictures of the happy couple. And *The Toronto Star*, one of Canada's biggest newspapers, said the ceremony had been a "compromise between the private service the couple wanted and the public nuptials expected of the Queen's third son". It added that the couple had "signalled that their marriage would break the mould of more grand, but ill-fated, royal weddings".

Below: The excited bridesmaids and pageboys ride through the town in a second Ascot carriage, together with Prince Charles and Prince Andrew.

Below: The two horse-drawn carriages sweep through the castle precincts and down to Windsor High Street, surrounded by jubilant crowds of well-wishers.

In Europe, the depth of coverage was mixed as France's *Le Monde* carried one story on the wedding, but *Der Spiegel* in Germany boasted a whole section of reports about the big day. Italy's *Corriere Della Sera* placed the wedding at the bottom of its front page and *El Pais* in Spain published a lengthy feature on the marriage. Further afield, *The Sunday Times* in South Africa headlined its story as a "Fairy-tale wedding that ends without a princess", referring to the couple taking the titles of Earl and Countess of Wessex.

As the honeymoon began, the wedding trade was moving into action, with a team of dressmakers racing against time to complete an exact replica of the royal wedding dress by the Monday morning after the wedding. Designer Helen Marina, an assistant designer, a cutter and two machinists, began work on the gown as soon as they saw Sophie on television. But they admitted they were worried about copying the dress's complicated beading. "Our team were concerned when they first saw it, but it is a challenge and they have risen to that challenge," a spokeswoman said. "They worked through the night and will probably stay up another night as well. It will be done on time. We will be using a beader – a woman who specializes in beading – and about 70 metres of beaded trim. We will have thousands of beads on our copy, though

not as many as Sophie had on her dress."

The sad news for brides-to-be is that the dress was a one-off that would not be sold, but was for display in Berkertex Brides in its central London store.

Also burning the midnight oil over Sophie were designers and dressers working for Madame Tussaud's. They, too, worked through the night to ensure that the wax figure of the Countess of Wessex was ready to be revealed to the public the day after the wedding – and eager royal watchers were queuing outside at 7am to be the first to catch a glimpse of the Countess in an exact replica of her wedding dress.

Sophie had sat for senior sculptor Stuart Williamson on three occasions while he modelled her in clay for the figure. And he said: "I really enjoyed modelling Sophie. She has a very interesting face. People say she looks like Diana, but the only thing I can see similar is the hair".

At first, the Countess was a little overwhelmed by the experience of being modelled for a waxwork, but seemed to be looking forward to her wedding day. He said: "She often referred to Edward and the wedding but only in a very general sense".

Sophie gave permission for an identical dress to be made by Samantha Shaw and when the dress is removed at the end of the year she will supply

Below: Escorted by the two red-coated postillions, a relaxed Edward and Sophie enjoy the good wishes of the gathered Windsor crowds.

19 JUNE 1999

26

STAMP OF APPROVAL

The Royal Mail's commemorative stamps celebrating the wedding of the year

19 June 1999

64

The engagement signalled the start of a rare race to produce commemorative stamps. "Usually we have up to 18 months on a project", says Royal Mail Design Director Barry Robinson, "but with the wedding forecast for late spring or early summer, we had to move fast".

Wednesday January 6, when the engagement was announced, was the starting-point, and the first step was to seek approval for a special issue from the Queen, head of the Royal Mail and owner of one of the world's greatest stamp collections. The royal collection has been lovingly nurtured over the generations, notably by King George V who, told by an aide that "some idiot" had paid a staggering sum for a stamp, replied: "Yes – that idiot was me!".

With royal approval received, the style of stamp was considered: "Photography rather than an artwork was our first choice", says Robinson, "because it's obviously the medium for capturing a moment in time, and for our deadline". John Swannell was commissioned to take the photographs for a 26p UK first-class stamp and a 64p airmail version. At 52 years of age, Swannell had photographed a catalogue of famous people, from Princess Anne, relaxed and reclining in a ballgown, to TV cook Delia Smith, up to her ears in pots and pans.

Above: The distinctive modern design and black-and-white photography of Edward and Sophie's stamps, reflects the couple's individuality and establishes their own break with past royal traditions.

Bottom left: The stamps' presentation pack also represents a departure from previous styling, with its contemporary typography and design replacing the traditional coats-of-arms and elaborate engravings.

On Saturday March 13, Swannell drove to Windsor to take the pictures: "That was the earliest Edward and Sophie could see me", he says, "but once we fixed the date they couldn't have been more helpful. I asked them to wear black polo-neck sweaters for a clean, uncluttered image, and they liked the idea. Royal wedding stamps usually mean bright colour, but I decided on black and white because it's stronger and more honest somehow. Royal Mail were slightly apprehensive, but Barry Robinson backed me all the way".

Swannell was given a room in Edward's apartment to work in. "But it was too small", he says, "so I ended up

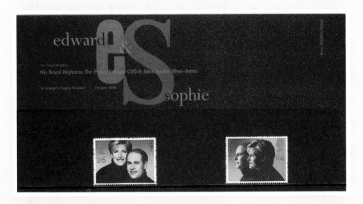

...king the pictures in a corridor. At one
...oint a door opened and a lady with
...orgis scampering at her feet – I think it
...as the Queen, though she was too far
...way to be sure – peered out. They all
...anted to know what was going on in
...eir corridor!".

A contemporary design

...y Monday morning, the best of the
...hotographs were on Barry Robinson's
...esk at Royal Mail's City of London
...eadquarters and he, Swannell and a
...ypographer began "composing" the
...amps, using the photos, obligatory
...utline of the Queen's head, values and
...aptions. The layouts were sent to the
...ouple, who were "very, very happy with
...em", and then to printers De La Rue
...High Wycombe in Buckinghamshire,
...here technical trials were done on
...olour mixtures, textures and contrasts.
...nd by Friday I had the first proofs of
...e proposed stamps", says Robinson.

"That afternoon I drove straight from
...e printers, to Edward's office at
...agshot and gave them to his private
...cretary, Lieutenant-Colonel Sean
...'Dwyer. He said: "They're magnifi-
...nt!", which was comforting, because
...the back of your mind is always the
...ought that if the stamps don't get
...pproval, you'd have to start all over
...gain". Soon after, Edward and Sophie
...eclared themselves equally "delighted"
...d the Queen's approval swiftly
...llowed. Work then started on first-day
...overs and presentation packs, "and
...ith the modern image approved, we
...ied to reflect it in these items",
...ys Barry Robinson, "with modern
...pography and design replacing the
...ore usual elaborate engravings and
...ats-of-arms".

On Monday April 12, De La Rue
...arted gravure-printing 55 million 26p
...amps and some 14 million of the 64p
...rsion, in the familiar sheets of 100.
...ey went straight to checkers, workers
...ho flick through vast volumes of
...amps to weed out any with the

smallest flaw – a dot, a smudge or
inking error which can add considerable
sums to a stamp's value. Once checked,
the stamps were delivered to the supply
depot at Hemel Hempstead in
Hertfordshire for distribution to the
Philatelic Bureau in Edinburgh – who
prepare the presentation packs and
first-day covers – and to 20,000 UK
Post Offices.

On Tuesday June 15, the stamps
went on sale. "I'm just one of a vast
army of people behind their
production", says Barry Robinson, "but
I'm sure we all get enormous
satisfaction when we see them on
envelopes. And I'm very happy with
these. They could so easily have been
rather stuffy and formal, but they're
strong and bold and modern, and could
well be a marker for the future".

John Swannell – who was also asked
to take private photographs of the
couple for the Queen and her family
while he was on his stamps project –
agrees. "Edward and Sophie have told
me they are thrilled with the result", he
says, "and I'm very happy, too. They are
a young, modern couple with a fresh
outlook and way of seeing things, and I
hope we've managed to portray that
with the stamps".

Top: Previous stamps celebrating the marriages
of Princess Anne, Prince Charles and Prince
Andrew, reflect changing styles over the years.

Above: Design Director Barry Robinson proudly
displays the first printed sheets of the Royal
Mail commemorative stamps.

Left: Distinguished British photographer
John Swannell is known for his portraits of
celebrities and TV personalities, as well as
members of the royal family.

Right: The landaus carrying the bride and groom, with Prince Charles and the bridesmaids behind, en route for the reception at the castle.

Opposite: An official wedding photograph of family and visiting dignitaries in the regal surroundings of Windsor Castle.

something from her own wardrobe. And the jewellery she wore on her wedding day was also being copied.

Diana Moon from Madame Tussaud's said: 'The people standing outside kept asking when we were opening and kept saying 'We want to see the dress'". And general manager Martin Westwood said: "We are expecting lots of interest from the public. This will be a unique opportunity for our guests to get right up close and examine every detail of this very special new addition to the exhibition".

The Earl and Countess of Wessex take centre stage in the royal family group in Madame Tussaud's Grand Hall. Hundreds of measurements and photographs were taken by Madame Tussaud's artists and the Countess's hands were even cast in wax for a perfect likeness. Every detail – down to

1 & 2 Mr & Mrs James Ogilvy, 3 & 4 The Count & Countess of Commarque, 5 Prince Philip of Hohenlohe-Langenburg, 6 Princess Xenia of Hohenlohe-Langenburg, 7 Prince Nikolaos of Greece, 8 Princess Rahma El-Hassan of Jordan, 9 Mr Alaa Batayneh of Jordan, 10 & 11 Princess Irina & Count Schonburg, 12 & 13 Lady Sarah & Daniel Chatto, 14 Lady Rose Windsor, 15 & 16 Timothy & Lady Helen Taylor, 17 & 18 Prince & Princess Joachim of Denmark, 19 Sir Angus Ogilvy, 20 The Duke of York, 21 Princess Alexandra, 22 & 23 Prince Hassan of Jordan and Princess Sarvath, 24 The Prince of Wales, 25 & 26 Princess & Prince Michael of Kent, 27 & 28 Prince & Princess Guillaume of Luxembourg, 29 The Crown Prince of Norway, 30 Peter Phillips, 31 The Queen of the Hellenes, 32 & 33 Zara Phillips & Prince of Asturias, 34 Pengiran Isteri (wife of Sultan of Brunei), 35 Sultan of Brunei, 36 Raja Isteri (Sultan's senior wife), 37 & 38 Duke & Duchess of Kent, 39 & 40 Edward & Sophie, 41 The Princess Royal, 42 Cdr Tim Laurence, 43 & 44 Duke & Duchess of Gloucester, 45 Prince Harry, 46 Prince William, 47 Princess Beatrice, 48 The Earl of Snowdon, 49 Princess Eugenie, 50 The Queen Mother, 51 The Duke of Edinburgh, 52 The Queen, 53 & 54 Christopher Rhys-Jones & wife Mary, 55 Prince George of Hanover, 56 Princess Margaret, 57 Camilla Hadden, 58 Felix Sowerbutts, 59 Harry Warburton, 60 Olivia Taylor

WHEN WE WERE YOUNG

*Sophie's family are happy to share loving memories of the daughter
who was to grow from a cheeky toddler to a titled lady*

On the day of her marriage, these private family pictures of Sophie, never before published, were released through Buckingham Palace. They record how the girl from Homestead Farmhouse grew from cheeky toddler through enthusiastic schoolgirl to a go-getting teenager with her first new car.

Never far away is the smile and the obvious love of laughter which enchanted the prince who would become her husband. It's there on the face of the impish toddler … as she poses playfully with her five-year-old brother David … in her school uniform as a seven-year-old … as a 10-year-old on a family holiday in Devon … and proudly showing off her new car, a bright red Morris Minor, in 1989.

For years they have been treasured family photographs, but as Sophie joined the most photographed family in the world, her parents decided to share them with the world.

Top: A favourite snap from the Rhys-Jones family album.
Above: Smiles for the camera during a Devon holiday.

Top: The proud owner of her first car, in 1989.
Above: A confident seven-year-old schoolgirl.
Right: Aged three, with brother David.

earrings, jewellery, make-up and the bouquet – was meticulously copied, and a sample of Sophie's hair was taken to match with supplies in Germany.

The public gave an enthusiastic reaction to the latest arrival. Among them was Teresa Buckfield, from Southend, Essex, who said: "I didn't expect a model of Sophie to be here so quickly. But I'd give it 10 out of 10 for realism – it's really quite lifelike".

As long as they'd got the eyes right, it would be perfect. For on this day of days, when the girl from Homestead Farmhouse at last married her prince, the eyes had said it all.

Now the newlyweds were keeping out of sight: when they'd left their reception they had not gone far. They drove to Royal Lodge to stay with the Queen Mother, and next morning set off for yet another party at their new Bagshot Park home – a "brunch" hosted by Sophie's parents. It was the morning-after-the-great-day-before and it was 11.20am before Edward, in casual slacks and shirt, drove his tee-shirted new bride through the gates of their mansion. They were followed soon afterwards by guests who included the Queen and Prince Philip, Princess Margaret, and Prince Andrew, driving daughters Beatrice and Eugenie in his open-topped, bottle-green Aston Martin.

The greatest mother in the world

The royals were joined by many of Sophie's relatives for the family affair brunch, during which guests spilled out on to Bagshot Park's manicured lawns to watch the Queen plant a weeping willow as a gift for the couple's new home. At his wedding reception, Edward had called her "the greatest mother in the world", and the Queen responded after planting the tree by saying a few informal words in praise of her son and his new bride. Next day there was another present from that wonderful mother, when it was announced that Edward's personal allowance from the Queen was to be increased from £45,000 to £141,000 to cover, it was said, "extra paperwork".

Presents were a big talking point: it was Prince William's 17th birthday, and he was given his first car. The prince, already a motorbike rider, chose a £15,000 VW Golf GT diesel and, keen to get his L-plates up and out on the road, he had already applied for a provisional driving licence.

As the brunch guests again toasted the couple with champagne, a helicopter was taking off from the small Blackbush airport, seven miles from

Above: A happy wave from Edward and a radiant smile from Sophie as their carriage takes them to the reception.

Bagshot, and heading for the mansion. When it landed, Edward and Sophie said a final farewell to their parents and guests, who waved them off as they left in the helicopter. It flew directly to Balmoral, where the couple had enjoyed some of the happiest moments of their courtship, and they drove on to Birkhall, the Queen Mother's favourite Scottish retreat.

It had the great advantage, especially for honeymooners, of being totally private, but many believed the newlyweds would stay in the often-bleak and windswept Highlands for just a day or two, before heading off somewhere a great deal warmer for a two-week break. Yet again, though, the unconventional couple sprang a surprise. It was widely reported that after a few days they would head back home and to work, and take a holiday later in the year.

Both Edward and Sophie had stressed how busy they are – fitting in a wedding had not helped their hectic schedules – and they decided it would be better to stay close to base, to keep an eye on business and the final work on their new home, rather than lying on a beach somewhere. That is most definitely not their style.

Edward Windsor and Sophie Wessex may have grand titles in their royal lives, but otherwise they remain a modern and enterprising career-minded young couple with new and individual ideas – as they showed with style and flair at a wedding that may set the pattern for many more in the years to come.

THE RHYS-JONES FAMILY'S

A new Rhys-Jones family tree and a restyled crest reveal Sophie's "blue-blood" links

Sophie Rhys-Jones discovered some fascinating facts about herself and her family only after she became engaged to Prince Edward – not least that she is a distant cousin of the Queen and the late Diana, Princess of Wales.

The Rhys-Joneses gave Robert Barrett, Research Editor of the *Daily Mail*, exclusive access to family papers which reveal Sophie's "blue-blood" link through her grandfather's 1928 marriage to Patricia Molesworth – a descendant of the first Viscount Molesworth, a 17th-century diplomat.

Sophie's Welsh ancestry is traced to the 11th-century warriors Elystan Glodrydd, Prince of Ferring, and his son Cadwagan. And her Irish links come through her mother's O'Sullivan family, who were farmers and shopkeepers around the area of Bantry in West Cork.

Robert Barrett, uncovering the family facts the day after the engagement announcement, revealed that Sophie's father Christopher "added the hyphen to his family name more than 30 years ago, he admits, 'because it sounded classier'".

But he was not the first in the family to tweak the name a little. It was also smartened up in the late 18th century by a leading freeman called Rice

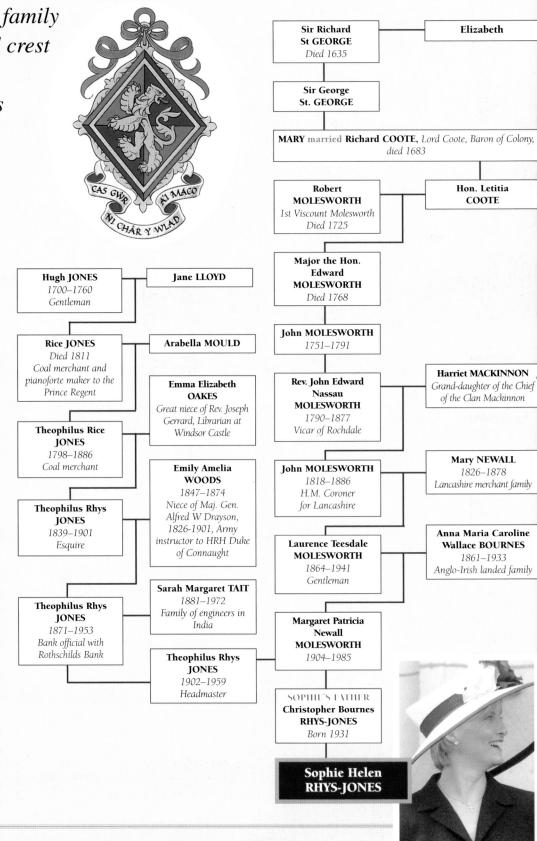

CAS GWR A'I MACO
NI CHÂR Y WLAD

Sir Richard St GEORGE *Died 1635* — **Elizabeth**

Sir George St. GEORGE

MARY married Richard COOTE, *Lord Coote, Baron of Colony, died 1683*

Robert MOLESWORTH *1st Viscount Molesworth Died 1725* — **Hon. Letitia COOTE**

Major the Hon. Edward MOLESWORTH *Died 1768*

John MOLESWORTH *1751–1791*

Hugh JONES *1700–1760 Gentleman* — **Jane LLOYD**

Rice JONES *Died 1811 Coal merchant and pianoforte maker to the Prince Regent* — **Arabella MOULD**

Emma Elizabeth OAKES *Great niece of Rev. Joseph Gerrard, Librarian at Windsor Castle*

Theophilus Rice JONES *1798–1886 Coal merchant*

Rev. John Edward Nassau MOLESWORTH *1790–1877 Vicar of Rochdale* — **Harriet MACKINNON** *Grand-daughter of the Chief of the Clan Mackinnon*

Emily Amelia WOODS *1847–1874 Niece of Maj. Gen. Alfred W Drayson, 1826-1901, Army instructor to HRH Duke of Connaught*

John MOLESWORTH *1818–1886 H.M. Coroner for Lancashire* — **Mary NEWALL** *1826–1878 Lancashire merchant family*

Theophilus Rhys JONES *1839–1901 Esquire*

Laurence Teesdale MOLESWORTH *1864–1941 Gentleman* — **Anna Maria Caroline Wallace BOURNES** *1861–1933 Anglo-Irish landed family*

Sarah Margaret TAIT *1881–1972 Family of engineers in India*

Theophilus Rhys JONES *1871–1953 Bank official with Rothschilds Bank*

Theophilus Rhys JONES *1902–1959 Headmaster*

Margaret Patricia Newall MOLESWORTH *1904–1985*

SOPHIE'S FATHER
Christopher Bournes RHYS-JONES *Born 1931*

Sophie Helen RHYS-JONES

YAL CONNECTIONS

Nicholas St JOHN
c 1526–1589

Sir John St JOHN
Died 1594

A TUDOR ROSE
Prince Edward's new badge was designed by Peter Gwynn-Jones at the Royal College of Arms, and incorporates a simple Tudor rose surrounded by Scottish thistles. Badges were first used on battlefields to identify knights and their followers, but Edward will be able to use his on stationery, cutlery, tea cups, furnishings, gifts and a lot more.

Barbara St JOHN
Died 1672
married
Sir Edward Villiers
Died 1626

Sir Edward Villiers
1620–1689

Frances (or Ann)
Died 1688
married
Hans W. BENTINCK
Earl of Portland
Died 1709

Henry
Duke of Portland
1682–1726

William
2nd Duke of Portland
1708/9–1762

William Henry
3rd Duke of Portland
1738–1809

Lord William CAVENDISH BENTINCK
1780–1826

Rev Charles CAVENDISH BENTINCK
1817–1865

Nina Cecilia
1862–1938
Countess of Strathmore

HM THE QUEEN MOTHER
Born 1900

HM THE QUEEN
Born 1926

Cornelius O'SULLIVAN
1828–1899
Postmaster
married
Agnes McFEELY
Died 1914

Daniel O'CONNOR
Died 1910
Police Inspector
married
Bridget POWER
Died 1914

Charles Henry STOKES
1847–1927
Cooper
married
Maria ARCHER
1849–1927

Alexander SAUNDERS
Boilermaker
married
Emma WEBSTER (nee LYNE)

Michael O'SULLIVAN
1867–1950
Telegraphist

Mary Ann O'CONNOR
1865–1940

George Frederick STOKES
1877–1948
Company Director

Emma SAUNDERS
1875–1963

Cornelius Thomas O'SULLIVAN
1896–1939
Bank Inspector

Doris Emma STOKES
1901–1984
Remarried Wing Commander Archie Drew

SOPHIE'S MOTHER **Mary** O'SULLIVAN
Born 1934

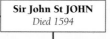

Prince EDWARD

Jones, who was the official musical instrument maker to the Prince of Wales, later George IV. He changed his first name of Rice to Rhys, "to make it sound more Welsh" and it remained a family forename until Sophie's father incorporated it into the family surname.

Now Sophie is part of the family to whom Windsor is home, and in keeping with her new role she was given a new family crest in May. Devised by Peter Gwynn-Jones, Garter Principal King of Arms at the College of Arms in London, the crest features a diamond quartered into the gules (red) and azure (blue) colours of the Royal Fusiliers, in which several members of the family served. A roaring golden lion represents the Welsh warriors in Sophie's family tree, and the motto, "Hateful the man who loves not the country that nurtured him", is written in Welsh.

Edward's own brand new badge, featuring Tudor rose and Scottish thistles, was granted to him by royal warrant just a week before the wedding. "The badge is a combination of historic royal badges", said the College of Arms, "but it is a unique design for the prince".

Picture Credits

All Action: 67, 68, 70b, 71t (Doug Peters), 72b (Mark Cuthbert), 73t (Mark Cuthbert), 80tl (Eamonn Clarke), 81 (Alan Davidson), 86bl (Doug Peters), 86br (Anwar Hussein), 99t

Alpha: 16b, 17, 25t, 30t (Randolf Caughie), 33t (Dave Chancellor), 33b (Dave Chancellor), 39t, 42t, 44bl, 44tr, 45b, 46, 55b, 56b (Richard Chambury), 57l (Richard Chambury), 57r (Richard Chambury), 60, 61t, 61b, 62 (Dave Chancellor), 65, 69 (Dave Benett), 71b (Dave Chancellor), 72c (Dave Chancellor), 75t, 75b (Steve Finn), 79b (Duncan Raban), 85t, 85b (Dave Benett), 88b (Dave Chancellor), 89 (Steve Finn), 90 (Steve Daniels), 94 (Richard Chambury), 95 (Dave Chancellor), 100b (Dave Benett), 101 (Dave Benett), 103, 107, 109t, 111t, 112l, 112r, 113t, 113c, 113b, 114t, 115, 116t, 116b, 117, 126b, 128, 129, 137, 138t, 139t, 139c

Anwar Hussein: 36t, 39b, 40l, 40r, 41bl, 41tr, 46c

AP: 134 (Findlay Kember)

Camera Press: 14r (Mark Stewart), 23t (Dorothy Wilding), 23b, 24b (Glenn Harvey), 26tl, 29t (Richard Open), 31t, 31b, 32 (Cecil Beaton), 36b, 37t (John Scott), 37b (Cecil Beaton), 38l (Joan Williams), 50, 53b (William Conran), 64, 66 (Mike Roberts), 72t (Ian Lloyd), 74 (Richard Gillard), 76 (Srdja Djukanovic), 84b (Srdja Djukanovic), 99b (Stewart Mark)

David Cheskin: 16t

Frank Spooner: 42b (Keith Butler), 83 (Paul Massey)

Geoffrey Shackerley: 135

Glenn Harvey: 48, 54bl

John Swannell: 133bl

Mirror Group Newspapers: 14l (Kent Gavin), 22, 28, 29b, 58, 59t, 59b, 82, 84t

Neil Sutherland (Quadrillion Publishing): 80br, 132t, 132c, 132b, 133cr

Press Association: 12/13, 15t, 18b, 19 (John Stillwell), 104-5 (Kent Gavin), 106, 107t, 108t, 108b, 110t, 110b, 111b, 114b, 115t, 118 (Jane Fincher), 119 (Jane Fincher, 120 (Jane Fincher), 121t (Jane Fincher), 121b (Jane Fincher), 122 (Ian Jones), 123 (John Stillwell), 126t (NewsPix International), 127, 130, 131 (Peter Jordan), 138b, 139b, 141

Photographers International: 78

Popperfoto: 38r

Prism Rights Ltd: 136 (all photographs © Prism Rights Ltd)

Private Collection: 51, 96, 97t, 97c, 97b

Reuters: 15b (Dylan Martinez), 109b (Ian Waldie)

Rex Features: 20 (Chris Harris), 45t (Nils Jorgensen), 47 (Graham Trott), 52, 53t, 55t, 56t, 70t, 79tr (Charles Sykes), 102 (Nils Jorgensen)

Royal Mail: 133tr

The Sun: 54t, 54br

Tim Graham: 24t, 25b, 26tr, 26b, 27, 30b, 34, 43, 73b, 79tl, 88t, 92, 93, 98, 100t

Tony Stone: 86t, 87t, 87b

Woodmansterne Ltd: 124t, 124b, 125t, 125bl, 125br

Key: L = LEFT, R = RIGHT, T = TOP; B = BOTTOM; C = CENTRE

EVERY EFFORT HAS BEEN MADE TO CONTACT COPYRIGHT HOLDERS IN EACH CASE. WE APOLOGIZE FOR ANY OMISSIONS.

Publisher's Acknowledgements

The publishers would like to thank Sean Smith for the invaluable help and advice he has given to the author and publishers of this book. Bookman Projects would also like to thank Ric Papineau of Mirror Group for his good offices (again).

Author's Acknowledgements

The author would like to thank again the many people who kindly took the time and trouble to give invaluable assistance in the preparation of this book.

Special thanks to: Malcolm Cockren and the staff of Ardent Productions; Geoff Crawford, Prince Edward's Press Secretary; Nigel Dempster of the *Daily Mail Diary*; Paul Jenkins for his help in America; Daphne Jones of Peter Jones China; Paul Massey; Brian MacLaurin and Amanda Lovejoy of the MacLaurin Group; Anne McCarthy of West Kent College, Tonbridge; Trevor Morris of the Quentin Bell Organisation; Lieutenant-Colonel Sean O'Dwyer, Private Secretary to Prince Edward; Suzanne O'Hare of Kent College, Pembury; Robin Peverett, former headmaster of Dulwich College Preparatory School, Cranbrook; Robin Pratt of The Halfway House, Brenchley; Tom Rhodes of *The Sunday Times* in America; Royal Mail's Barry Robinson and Matthew Eastley; Robin Simons of Meridian Television; John Swannell; Keith Waterhouse; James Whitaker of *The Mirror*; Egerton Shelswell White of Bantry House, Bantry, West Cork; and in Windermere Island, Bahamas, Jackie Kemp and Ricardo Bovero, and Julie Angove of the Bahamas Tourist Office.

Thanks also to the authors whose work is briefly quoted: Robin Eggar, *Commando: Survival of the Fittest* (John Murray, 1994); Garth Gibbs and Sean Smith, *Sophie's Kiss* (Blake Publishing, 1997); Elizabeth Longford, *Royal Throne: The Future of the Monarchy* (Hodder, 1993); and Ingrid Seward, *Prince Edward: A Biography* (Century, 1995).